TRAINING IN LOGISTICS AND THE FREIGHT TRANSPORT INDUSTRY

Training in Logistics and the Freight Transport Industry

The experience of the European Project ADAPT-FIT

Edited by
GENNARO FERRARA
Università degli Studi di Napoli 'Parthenope'
ALFONSO MORVILLO
CNR-IRAT, Italy

ASHGATE

Published by
Ashgate Publishing Limited
Gower House
Croft Road
Aldershot
Hampshire GU11 3HR
England

Ashgate Publishing Company
131 Main Street
Burlington, VT 05401-5600 USA

Ashgate website: http://www.ashgate.com

British Library Cataloguing in Publication Data
Training in logistics and the freight transport industry : the
        experience of the European project ADAPT-FIT. - (Transport
        and mobility series)
        1. Freight and freightage - Italy - Management 2. Business
        logistics - Italy 3. Transport workers - Training of - Italy
        I. Ferrara, Gennaro II. Morvillo, Alfonso
        388'.044'0687

Library of Congress Control Number: 2002102834

ISBN 0 7546 1762 9

Typeset in South Africa by Martingraphix
Printed and bound in Great Britian by MPG Books Ltd,
Bodmin, Cornwall.

Contents

List of Figures

List of Tables

List of Contributors

Valentina Carbone	Junior Researcher at Institute of Service Industry Research – IRAT/CNR, Naples, Italy
Marcella De Martino	Junior Researcher at Institute of Service Industry Research – IRAT/CNR, Naples, Italy
Pietro Evangelista	Researcher at Institute of Service Industry Research – IRAT/CNR, Naples, Italy
Gennaro Ferrara	Rector of University of Naples 'Parthenope' and President of Scientific Board of IRAT/CNR, Naples, Italy
Antonio Minguzzi	Researcher at University of Molise, Campobasso, Italy
Alfonso Morvillo	Senior Researcher at Institute of Service Industry Research – IRAT/CNR, Naples, Italy
Immacolata Vellecco	Senior Researcher at Institute of Service Industry Research – IRAT/CNR, Naples, Italy

Foreword

In this book we seek to illustrate the experience made in the past three years at the Institute for Service Industry Research (IRAT) of the National Research Council and University of Naples 'Parthenope', through an intensive training and research activity implemented within the Transnational Integrated Training Project (FIT-Formazione Integrata Transnazionale).

The FIT Project, funded by the European Programme ADAPT, is a joint action implemented by the academic, research and entrepreneurial world to boost the Transport and Logistic Industry in southern Italy. The aim of the project is to offer a solution to the rising needs of professionalism and flexibility in this sector through innovative, modular training.

This sector is undergoing innovative strategic, organisational and management processes, which are challenging the effectiveness of current skills from the decisional and operational standpoint. The extensive diffusion of Information and Communication Technology (ICT) has also introduced new factors of complexity. These new factors have a major impact on sectors with an entrepreneurial culture greatly affected by company size, by growing internationalisation and, in general, by the lack of stimuli from the external environment which drive the growth process.

The aims of this volume are:

♦ to illustrate the structural aspects of the logistics and transport industry in southern Italy with respect to increasing training needs;
♦ to illustrate an innovative methodological framework to manage training processes;
♦ to disseminate the outcome of the project in the logistics and transport industry, presenting its operational guidelines as 'best practices'.

The book consists of two parts. In the first part the structural features of the logistics and freight transport industry in Italy are illustrated and the resulting training needs are highlighted. In the second part training methodologies and process management are dealt with and FIT results are presented. The appendix includes a collection of Web-sites related to European training institutions performing in the reference sector.

In particular the first chapter illustrates the innovative elements which have characterised the sector in past years, with a specific focus on the Italian case. The ways in which the evolutionary dynamics of demand for logistics and transport services have affected supply structure and development strategies are highlighted. An analysis is also made of the impact generated by the supply of logistics and transport services on the value chain in manufacturing firms. At the end of this introductory chapter, the main implications for the training needs of the industry are outlined.

The second chapter focuses on the role of ICT on advanced logistics and supply chain management. The effects of these new technologies on the activities performed by logistics and transport service providers are also analysed with a specific view to the Italian case. In the final part some policy measures are suggested to train and develop new professional skills. Using ICT has become a pre-requisite to perform effectively in the sector.

In the third chapter training services for the Italian industry are analysed. After outlining the recent main training strategies adopted by Italian public institutions, attention is focused on the new training provided to meet the present needs. An interesting and new scenario is outlined which shows how, despite the wide range of training services provided, additional efforts have to be made for constant adjustment to increasingly changing needs.

In the fourth chapter a detailed analysis is made of the logistics and transport service market in Italy – and specifically in southern Italy – aimed at understanding the specific context which is the target of the training activity. From the methodological standpoint, the analysis is based upon both bibliographic sources and an empirical survey conducted through administration of a questionnaire to a representative sample of firms.

The fifth chapter of the book, which concludes its first part, is focused on the relationships between cultural profiles of southern Italian entrepreneurs and dissemination of ICT in firms. A theoretical model is used which evaluates the impact of the various *cross-country*, *cross-industry* and *cross-firm* factors on ICT dissemination. The analysis highlights that the impact generated by cross-country and cross-firm factors is substantially higher than the impact generated by sector variables. This is an important result for the development of proper training policies as it highlights that their effectiveness is not substantially correlated to the sector involved.

In the sixth chapter, which opens the second part of the book, the basic guidelines of the training project are illustrated, highlighting its innovative elements, namely flexibility and personalisation of the individual training path.

Chapter 7 deals with the analysis of training needs, an analysis viewed both as a tool for labour and employment policies at European level and as a planning tool to support training operators. After illustrating the features of the different systems adopted in Europe to anticipate training needs, with specific reference to the Italian system, the chapter investigates the main approaches and tools being developed when designing a strategy to analyse training needs within the framework of a training project. Lastly the application of the training needs analysis, tested within the FIT Project, is suggested.

In chapter 8, mainly dealing with methodology, a theoretical analysis of the most widespread models for training evaluation is illustrated. This analysis sets out to identify the most suitable systemic model for the FIT characteristics. The tools of the identified model and the outcome of the evaluation process are then illustrated.

We feel several points are worth underlining. First, for reasons mainly of space, the subject matter has been somewhat restricted: the book should not be considered a manual on training in general or a global overview of training phases, given that the subject has already received extensive coverage in the literature. What we have sought to do is provide a significant contribution to elaborating a training approach for small and medium enterprises working in the logistics and freight transport sector, being fully aware that large players in the sector are able to assess their own training needs and choose the most suitable approaches.

We therefore overlooked some of the general aspects of training, and opted instead to cover aspects that are peculiar to training in the demand segment chosen. In effect, this choice represents the book's innovation. In this respect, three distinct elements can be identified:

♦ application to the Transport and Logistics Industry of innovative methodology to analyse training needs, which also sets out the standard professional profiles of the industry (*Methodological innovation*);
♦ impact of research outcome on entrepreneurial culture and Information Technology diffusion in SMEs (*Knowledge*);
♦ guide to select Transport and Logistics Training Institutions through Web sites (*Working tool*).

The training-research initiative carried out within the target industry highlighted the profound differences existing in the sector in terms of culture, motivation to participate in training and training needs. This implies that training requires two different strategies: one strategy addressed to firms not yet aware of the importance of training (e.g. shipping agents, forwarders, etc.), and another strategy addressed to those firms which have already developed considerable interest and have already invested in training (shipping companies, road hauliers). The first strategy should aim to make operators aware of the strategic role played by training, providing them with 'information' rather than 'training'. The second strategy should aim to improve training methods and work on contents.

   This book is mainly addressed to personnel managers in logistics and transport firms, and those working with European training and research institutions, as well as National and European Entrepreneur Associations. Our comments and analysis will be particularly relevant to trainers, training managers and all those involved with training in logistics and freight transport. This experience may be identified as an example of best practices in the training context, with significant elements concerning:

♦ strategies adopted to achieve objectives of employability, professionalism and partnership-building;
♦ the quality of in-house and external resources;
♦ Reproducibility and transferability of the project structure.

The aim of the project was to create proper conditions for job flexibility, in other words the capability of the labour force to perform different functions both within the same firm and in other firms of the logistics chain. Such an ambitious aim is of key importance given the far-reaching changes affecting the logistics and freight transport sector, especially in Italy where this process started later than in other countries.

   To achieve this objective, we chose to adopt an adaptive project strategy, which consists in original ways to develop experience able to enhance the match between the professional skills supplied and the professional skills required. The strategy adopted is based on original approaches to training that aim to reconcile two contrasting needs: on the one hand, to fill the training gap emerging during the pre-training/orientation phase and, on the other, to allow for the low time availability on the part of participants who are generally employed in small firms. The adoption of a flexible modular system that allows personalisation of each training path is undoubtedly an innovative method, at least in the sector in question.

Implementation of the project strategy (research, orientation, training) was conceived in integrated fashion, thereby making the FIT project a 'research-intervention' programme rather than just a training course, with considerable impact on the context in question in terms of greater awareness of the importance of training in a sector where *learning by doing* remains the dominant approach for skills development.

PART I

TRAINING IN LOGISTICS AND FREIGHT TRANSPORT: BACKGROUND

Chapter 1

Trends in Logistics and Freight Transport in Italy: Implications on Training Needs

Alfonso Morvillo

Introduction

The issues related to training in the transport industry should be supported by a thorough analysis of the strategic and innovative elements that have marked the evolution of freight transport. Since the demand for transport is of a derived type, structural modifications in the sector are influenced by significant changes which have affected the manufacturing and distribution processes.

The globalisation of sourcing and consumer markets, the decentralisation of production, the concentration of warehouses and distribution centres and just-in-time have made the economic system highly transport-intensive. Indeed, in the last few decades the role of transport in the context of production processes has grown considerably, above all in Western countries. More recently, in the light of innovations relating to the development of Information and Communication Technologies (ICT), the concept of transport has gone further in the widest sense of logistics.

Transport facilitates the flow of materials between diverse nodal points in the logistics cycle of the manufacturing firm, in three separate stages: inbound, internal and outbound. While on the one hand its economic importance is reduced because of lower costs and greater strategic weight is given to other logistics activities, on the other hand the impact of just-in-time has increased its importance.

Just-in-time forces companies to produce and deliver exclusively in 'response to demand', with the aim of reducing stocks and, hence, lead time along the entire logistics chain. To this end, timing in raw materials' supply for production purposes and the delivery of finished goods becomes fundamental. The time factor is crucial and, consequently, so is transport (de Langen, 1999). Reliability, flexibility and frequency are increasingly viewed as critical success factors in transport which, in turn, influences the quality of supply and production time, and also how the service is perceived by customers.

On the supply side, the transport system is becoming increasingly complex, with more and more agents and activities interacting to ensure the swift and efficient flow of freight. Within this context, what emerges is that the business philosophy adopted by firms on the demand side is also undergoing radical change. Traditionally, relations between supply and demand were steered by the concept of effectiveness, and the objective of the transport operator was to manage freight handling according to the contractual terms (time delivery, costs, etc.). Today, there is greater complexity in the demand for transport, in the sense that logistics services other than transport are widely required. This has led to dramatic changes in the negotiations and contractual relations between shipper and carrier. Service efficiency, including all its components, is gaining ever-increasing significance.

The aim is therefore to offer a service which integrates the whole supply-production-distribution cycle by including support activities and managing the information flow, with a view to minimising costs in the logistics chain. Thus, the more complex the system becomes, the greater the need for transport operators who are professionally trained and are capable of understanding and managing the ever-changing demands of the market.

The Role of Logistics in the Transformation of Transport Business

The first logistics approaches were adopted by manufacturing and commercial firms of mass consumer goods, where logistics costs tended to have a high impact on total running costs. Subsequently, they were extended to other firms on the strength of the following factors (Ferrozzi *et al.*, 1985):

◆ a higher number of products and increased competition, leading to greater attention to consumer needs and the quality of service;
◆ globalisation of markets and decentralisation of production;
◆ stock reduction for just-in-time and gradual movement upstream of stocks, with a consequent increase in logistics problems;
◆ technological innovations in the field of ICT and transport which have lowered management costs of physical and information flows. Lower transport costs, together with stock reduction, have made the economic system progressively transport-intensive.

In the 1960s, as a result of the increased number of references and the fall in demand, company strategy focused on sales and on physical distribution. It was here that the conceptualisation of logistics began, though it was limited to the management of warehouses and deliveries to customers (outgoing transport). The crisis of the 1970s, which led to the rise in the cost of raw materials, highlighted the importance of procurements. Accordingly, the concept of logistics as a cross-function became increasingly significant in the search for efficiency, not only in distribution but also in procurements and production. The intense global competition of the 1980s forced companies to pursue the quality differential factor of products and services. In this respect, logistics moves from a tactical (cost optimisation) to a strategic role, adding value to products via service elements. Finally, from the 1990s onwards, the mission of companies has focused on the creation of value for the customers, giving rise to the need for the integration of logistics activities in a system designed to achieve both efficiency and effectiveness.

Logistics, therefore, has taken on a cross-functional role which, in making use of ICT, co-ordinates different company functions which until then were complementary yet separately managed (Stevens, 1989). The concept of integrated logistics begins to assert itself first in large enterprises, and then in smaller ones. The systemic and integrated approach of logistics becomes widespread and leads to the development of the concept of *Supply Chain Management* (SCM).

According to this approach, integration goes beyond the single company to include all the companies in the supply chain, from the raw materials supplier to the end consumer, with a view to identifying and exploiting the integrated management capability of the activities along the entire chain. In other words, the actors involved (suppliers, producers and distributors) converge in a single chain, the final aim of which is to provide customers with high value added products, services and information (Christopher, 1992).

SCM, therefore, is an even wider concept than logistics itself; it concerns not only the logistics process of a firm but all the organisations that take part in the management of the chain flows and related processes (Schary and Larsen, 1995).

SCM can be seen as a network of firms which interact to provide the final customer with the product and/or required service. Its aim is to manage the flow of goods and information along the chain in an integrated way so that possible synergies between operators may be exploited and unnecessary, unproductive and duplicated activities may be avoided. The actors along the chain forego their own competitiveness in favour of mutual collaboration so as to achieve shared overall objectives.

In this sense, then, far from being an added cost, logistics is part of a process whose aim is to ensure the delivery to the final consumer of a defined product, incorporating specific qualitative-quantitative features, such as availability (the product is there when it is needed) and quality of handling (packaging, post-manufacturing, kitting, etc.); these attributes are increasingly important in competitive terms.

A process has therefore been activated, encouraging innovation among both manufacturers and retailers (essentially, these form the market for logistics demand) and transport firms (essentially, these form the market for logistics supply).

An efficient logistics organisation presupposes a thorough knowledge not only of the theory of organisation, economics and national economy but also of the needs and constraints which affect the single components in the system. Indeed, logistics means above all integration. It integrates activities steering the flows of goods, services and information both along the production chain, so making products and services available on consumer markets, and along the transport chain, thereby facilitating the physical transfer of such goods from one place to another and, ultimately, to the final destination.

The development of systemic innovation concerns increasingly less the production cycle itself, and opens up relations with the end consumer market; not only do rules need to be agreed upon with the other actors in the chain, but at times the rules are imposed by the actor with the greatest bargaining power. In addition, the more logistics becomes the logistics of distribution, the more delicate becomes the management of so-called *physical distribution*, that is, the transport phase where the company's system of rules and relations must take into account the public domain, e.g. making use of the public infrastructure, as well as services often managed by public institutions.

Finally, logistics tends to become a tool for production planning and, as such, the most important factor of innovation in transportation, imposing homogeneous standards and selecting firms able to accept the new model through radical restructuring. Hence, transport companies incapable of adjusting to this framework are destined to become marginalised or forced to disappear.

It is precisely the system of freight transport which is being absorbed by logistics. The specific habits, uses and regulations of single transport means, as well as their practices and cultures, are being overturned by new organisation models that introduce selection criteria for competitive services and firms.

Outsourcing of Logistics Services and the Emergence of a New Industry

Within the process described above, the push towards modernisation of transport services stems from logistics outsourcing which consists in the gradual externalisation of logistics activities (primary transport, final distribution, warehousing, order processing, etc.) to a new typology of service provider, that is *logistics service provider*.

Outsourcing transforms the marginal and non-strategic activity of a firm into the main activity of another firm, providing the former with substantial cost reduction, greater focus on its *core business*, higher operational flexibility, increased efficiency of its externalised activities and better service levels. Furthermore, logistics outsourcing has a considerable impact on the product value and, finally, on the value of the company. Some research findings have shown that until recently the weight of logistics costs on total running costs was on the increase because of, among other factors, the globalisation of markets (McKinnon, 1999).

As a result of an increased tendency to resort to the outsourcing of strategic services close to the *core business*, the nature of supply is being modified through the adoption of a *demand pull* strategy. In particular, in response to demand needs, large transport operators have gradually broadened their business by controlling wider segments of the chain, combining different transport modes and supplying additional services such as warehousing, packaging, labelling, customs clearance and insurance. It is therefore possible to delineate a new market segmentation based on the degree of business complexity, in other words the greater or lesser ability of transport companies to respond to global demand.

At the first stage of complexity we find unimodal operators (i.e. companies that carry out a specific activity and/or function within the transport cycle) who tend to pursue niche strategies. At the second stage are the multimodal operators (i.e. companies that intervene in more steps or activities of the transport cycle) who possess a wider portfolio of services and can therefore satisfy multiple demand needs. The third stage includes *door-to-door* operators (i.e. companies that can organise, manage and control the freight from origin to final destination) who are increasingly in demand by shippers, giving rise to outsourcing even within the transport sector where supply relations between unimodal or multimodal operators (suppliers) and integrated transport operators (customers) are being generated. The fourth level of complexity covers firms that are capable not only of providing transport, but can also manage significant components of customers' logistics. This implies that operational and planning interrelationships between transport, procurement, production and distribution of products are becoming closer, to the extent that manufacturers outsource the organisation of inbound and outbound flows as well as the management of added value logistics activities to logistics providers.

The result of this transformation is that entry barriers of the logistics services sector are now higher, not only because of the substantial level of financial resources required but also due to the type of *know-how* needed. Indeed, in many segments of the transport and logistics market, such entry barriers are critical for those 'country-systems' (i.e. national economic systems) characterised by small and medium sized enterprises.

Moreover, logistics outsourcing presupposes a very high level of co-operation between customers and service suppliers (Bowersox, 1990; Gentry, 1993). In the context of partnership, the customer fixes the service standards but has to be in a position to control all operations at any moment. The logistics services supplier, on the other hand, is no longer merely the executive arm of the customer but plans and oversees the inbound and outbound freight flows in the numerous nodes of the logistics network, is responsible for improvements to the service levels and manages inventories and order processing, etc. (Cooper *et al.*, 1998). Hence, in order to develop specialised services, logistics providers have to broaden their own competencies in ICT in addition to their traditional logistics competencies.

Transport Infrastructures in the Italian '*country-system*'

The process of radical transformation and innovation, which in the last few years has marked the logistics and freight transport sector, has also had a substantial impact on the models of territorial use. In effect, the latter have privileged specialisation in some areas (so-called logistics districts) through the establishment of logistics and distribution platforms.[1] In terms of the transport chain, these platforms – located close to transport demand sites, ports, airports or road and rail interchanges – attract existing traffic and, furthermore, generate new traffic.

In the context of this new type of logistics structure, freight arriving on standard unit loads is transferred onto large road vehicles and delivered directly to the final customer, thereby eliminating both the through terminal passage and the following transfer to warehouses, from where the goods are delivered to customers. Consequently, traditional State-owned infrastructures (ports, airports, rail depots, etc.) carry out the straightforward operations such as transit, where loads remain stationed for the shortest time possible. Logistics, therefore, gives rise to the phenomenon of territorial hierarchisation between regions that enjoy significant competitive advantage deriving from the provision of logistics services and regions which, though showing levels of excellence in manufacturing industries, are weaker than the former in terms of integrated logistics services.

This aspect introduces another important concept. It has already been observed that production reorganisation requires logistics structures to be adapted to the demand for services. Similarly, the infrastructural supply network represented by new logistics systems might have a determining role in the reconfiguration of global value chains of manufacturing firms.

The problem of territorial logistics specialisation and interdependence with production systems should be interpreted in the light of social and legislative transformations peculiar to each country. This is why States and supranational institutions have accelerated the removal of many normative barriers which previously protected the transport sector. Transport deregulation in the United States at the beginning of the 1980s, and later in the European Union, has had very high social costs, yet has eradicated obstacles to the introduction of new models in transport firms.

In the last few years, in Europe for example, the main legal provisions relating to transport policies have adhered to the two fundamental principles of subsidiarity and non-discrimination. The former implies that the European Union will only intervene where interests prevail over those of single States; non-discrimination dictates that national policies do not conceal protectionist ends. Thanks to these measures, there has been a drastic reduction in transport costs in just a few years.

In short, knowledge of logistics and transport systems, together with their changing patterns, is crucial for logisticians in manufacturing and transport firms in their drive to become competitive. In actual fact, for firms, transport and logistics act as dependent and independent variables. The former refers to transport and logistics as functions to be optimised and, to this end, decision-makers have to know how to control the costs of single segments in the logistics chain, and how to choose the alternatives available on the market. The latter variable applies to transport and logistics systems viewed as constraints affecting the efficiency of the supply chain and the competitiveness of the firm and, ultimately, of the 'country-system' as a whole.

Information Technologies in Logistics and Freight Transport

The numerous applications of information technologies in transport and logistics at an international level may be traced back to the following needs:

♦ technical and operational integration among the actors along the supply chain;
♦ speed and timeliness in the transmission of shipment documents;
♦ monitoring and control of flows at the global level (tracing and tracking);
♦ computerisation of warehousing and distribution;
♦ selling services via telematic networks (e-commerce).

In particular, the development of ICT and the use of the Internet in business plays an important role in the process of transformation and innovation, which marks the sector of logistics operators. The most significant effects of e-commerce and e-business on demand for logistics services are as follows:

♦ fragmentation of orders for and deliveries of goods purchased on the Web, as a result of a higher number of consignees and greater personalisation;
♦ time extension for delivery of goods in urban areas;
♦ lowering of average order cycle times;
♦ increased number of international transactions.

The above effects broaden the phenomenon of external logistics outsourcing for manufacturing firms. Possible applications stemming from ICT improve the operational flexibility of firms and enable them to respond to the changing needs of demand. Furthermore, Internet potentialities facilitate logistics and freight transport firms so as to enrich their range of services with innovative ones, such as portal management for freight distribution, management of online freight auctions, monitoring of goods in the various stages of the chain and logistics management.

One of the most visible forms of integration between e-commerce and logistics systems is that of virtual platforms. The possibility of optimising stocks and reducing purchasing and procurement costs via access to inter-firm information systems (virtual warehouses) may be of particular interest, especially to SMEs.[2] In reality, however, it is precisely SMEs (particularly industrial districts, in the Italian context) that lag behind in the use of ICT for the purpose of increasing their own development potentialities. One of the main reasons for this delay lies in the fact that they prefer to maintain management autonomy (considered an irreplaceable source of flexibility), which accounts for their reluctance to share critical information about their markets with direct competitors. Moreover, establishing shared logistics platforms implies high investment costs, which are difficult to recover when strategic changes are adopted by the single firm.

Virtual logistics platforms, of course, overcome this obstacle. Indeed, it is not necessary to build a shared warehouse to optimise stocks and procurements; rather, it is sufficient to delegate information management of stock levels and order processing to a specialised provider. While not all procurement categories can be managed in this way, for many types of purchase and commodity procurements such a model is feasible. One condition for success is that those firms opting for a shared platform embrace a logistics-communication standard.

With regard to the typology and quality of logistics services required for e-commerce, the role of the logistics operator tends increasingly to become that of the organiser and integrator of various phases in a process starting from e-transaction and ending with the delivery of the product. This is clearly reflected in the ever-widening range of competencies and abilities required from the technological and organisational points of view. Furthermore, in the new e-commerce and e-business configuration, the territorial domain of logistics activities is enlarged, since the virtual market, i.e. the place where supply and demand for goods meet, becomes global.[3]

Logistics integrators, together with new operators whose target is either a specific chain or a market niche in need of highly specialised services, therefore become the actors who can best satisfy the new competitive conditions imposed by e-commerce. In this context, the large international operators, highly diversified and integrated throughout the entire logistics process (from freight management to freight transport), appear to have gained most from the relationship between e-commerce and the logistics sector.

Specific Features of Freight Transport and Logistics in Italy

The Italian position in the international context and the overall picture of freight transport has been traditionally marked by asymmetry between demand and supply.

Although it is ranked prominently among the group of industrialised countries with a high level of import-export trade, Italy shows signs of severe 'transport weakness', as demonstrated by progressive worsening in the transport balance of payments. This is the result of a persistent conservative transport policy that has for a long time prevented the sector from developing in line with evolutionary trends at the European level. Besides, the widespread demand for simple transport has not generated those stimuli that elsewhere have fostered the dynamism and innovation of value added services within the sector (Evangelista, Morvillo, 2000).

In the light of these considerations, the structures and features of the sector may be summarised thus:

♦ high level of fragmentation in supply, where companies adopt 'competitive positioning strategies based on territorial focus (local and regional markets), standard and operational services (hauliers), and in so doing are not able to satisfy the need for integration deriving from the more advanced sectors of demand' (Carrara, Monticelli, 1998);
♦ profound inadequacy of infrastructures, management, organisation and, more generally, of service quality. In particular, the lack of infrastructures slows down the expansion of the more advanced areas in Italy and inhibits, in the more backward areas, processes of development necessary for bridging severe territorial gaps;
♦ until ten years ago, little interest was expressed in the Italian market by more advanced foreign firms, thus depriving the sector of an important stimulus to competitiveness; at the same time, Italian companies were poorly equipped in skills terms to extend the scope of their own interest in foreign markets (Morvillo 2000; Federtrasporto, 2001);
♦ widespread adoption at decisional and operative levels of a transport culture that is not receptive to change and, at any rate, is still unaware of the importance of transport in the national economy.

As a consequence, in part, of the process of deregulation triggered in Europe, in the last few years transport policies in Italy have shown greater sensitivity to the needs stemming from the world of logistics and intermodality. In this respect, certain measures have been approved that are potentially capable of exerting a positive influence on the competitiveness of Italy.[4]

In line with what has happened in other more advanced countries, a radical restructuring process of the sector has begun in Italy, the impact of which has modified traditional borders and competition (Morvillo, 2000; Federtrasporto, 2001). In this sense, concentration and vertical integration already in progress should be interpreted as the result of merger and acquisition operations.

One remarkable aspect of the phenomenon in question is the unprecedented interest shown by foreign operators in the Italian market throughout the 1990s (Morvillo 2000; Federtrasporto 2001). This process is not likely to abate in the short term, largely because of the potential for development of the Italian market which, nonetheless, still lags behind.

To complete the picture outlined so far, it may be appropriate to draw attention to the barycentric position of Italy in the Mediterranean basin, making it a suitable candidate for the important role of logistics platform, at the service of economies and distribution markets in Northern Italy and Central Europe. Development of these trade routes points in two directions:

♦ North-South trade route: Italy is ideally positioned for the transfer of goods from South-East Asia to Central Europe through the Suez Canal; at the same time Italy is the major junction for European and Middle-Eastern/ North-African countries;
♦ East-West trade route: commercial trade between West and East-European countries is already in place and will continue to increase further in the future due to the enlargement of EU to East European countries.

Against this evolving background emerges the potential for a regional logistics area in Italy as well as new roles for local operators which, nevertheless, will only develop if certain stringent conditions are met:

♦ the logistics area must not become a heterogeneous complex of infrastructures, each of which is weak in its own competitive section (ports, aeroports and interports);
♦ a certain degree of integration (infrastructural and especially at the level of services) is fundamental if it is to be viewed as a multifunctional and multiservice platform at an international level;
♦ transport operators must be reconfigured as specialised logistics operators who are able to provide complex and high value added services.

Road haulage has undergone profound and urgent requalification precisely as a result of a widening logistics market which requires efficient, modern and *eco-compatible* vehicles, drivers trained to carry out auxiliary operations, satellite control systems, telematic interfaces with customers, regular and punctual services and deliveries, price transparency, greater carrier liability and geographical coverage at the European level. Once the above are in place and the initial stage is complete, it then becomes vital to know how to manage the extremely difficult maturity phase.

As far as rail transport is concerned, current difficulties within the system should be interpreted in the light of the delicate transition phase that other rail networks have already faced but not always solved in positive terms. This refers especially to streamlining relationships with associated companies, privatising State-owned railway companies, building alliances with other European operators and accepting market conditions, thereby eliminating the practice of subsidiarity.

Similarly, the system of maritime-port services faces a stabilising phase to be entirely based on value added services and distribution in addition to links with *inland terminals* of European networks. Competitiveness is no longer centred on berths, on handling services and, perhaps, not even on the port itself, but on the port hinterland in both geographical and virtual terms.

Training as a New Source for Competitive Advantage

The background described above highlights the salient features of a process that is still in progress, and is characterised by a determined drive towards innovation in terms of demand (manufacturing and retailing companies) and supply of transport and logistics services (providers, infrastructures, telematic networks).

In order to maximise the potential of this new production model and to explore new business opportunities, it is necessary to innovate company organisation and processes and, hence, new competencies and organisational behaviour at all levels. The nature of work itself changes in organisations: management by process, delegation, team work, network structure and project work require greater responsibility and involvement of highly competent and motivated collaborators, supported by clear guidelines and values stated by the company leadership.

With specific reference to Italy, it is worth describing beforehand some of the factors which call for newly-shaped competencies and knowledge in the sector, in such a way that a framework may become available for directing ideas and proposals and identifying objectives, targets and suggestions for policy makers.

The first step lies in focusing on the critical points which determine the transformation processes of a system that in Italy has only recently begun to free itself from those features of protectionism that have characterised it for so long. In this sense, Italy's integration with other European countries is fundamental.

The second step refers increasingly to the market (outsourcing) which stimulates the transformation of organisational models and cultural foundations necessary for change (Ministero dei Trasporti e della Navigazione, 2000).

It is likely that new rules and the market itself will provide the basic elements to bring about, within the many types of organisations operating in the transport sector, two processes in the specific area of human resources:

♦ the creation and dissemination of new professional figures in new activities and technologies;
♦ re-qualification and retraining of existing professional figures whose traditional configuration is no longer adequate for the current work context.

Until some years ago, those responsible for logistics in firms tended to be the same people in charge of the purchasing department. Later, with the introduction of just-in-time systems, production planners began to take on a decisive role in strategic choices together with the marketing department. The process of creating specific roles for logistics, and subsequently heads of logistics, in company organisational charts has been long and is still in progress. Greater specialisation seems necessary in the field of transport, relatively neglected so far, because the knowledge content for logisticians in the last few years has expanded to include inventory management and co-ordination between production planning and marketing functions.

Future training programmes for the creation and re-qualification of job profiles and competencies, while determining training content and teaching methodologies, will have to take into account the need to mix the specialist and transversal components.

Two distinct types of training needs can therefore be identified. Of the two, the priority is to develop specialist and horizontal competencies in existing professional resources (mostly at managerial and executive levels). The second type, on the other hand, is intended for those who will soon be called to carry out managerial and operative roles in public organisations as well as in transport and logistics companies.

The world of transport and logistics companies is becoming gradually more complex and segmented due to the specialisation of single operators and is shaping 'micro-cultures' that are often isolated from each other. Generally speaking, five key considerations emerge that are specific to human resources in transport:

♦ strategic and managerial decisions are usually taken by a restricted group of people who tend to identify with the head of the company (especially in SMEs);
♦ specialised competencies is very important at all levels and is particularly so up to the second and third hierarchical levels;
♦ pure professional figures are virtually non-existent in practice owing to the frequent overlapping of competencies and activities, especially in SMEs;
♦ technical knowledge, one of the core competencies for personnel in transport, requires new conceptual input as a result of technological innovation that is not acquired simply by doing;
♦ complex managerial abilities, other than implicit technical knowledge, are increasingly needed at middle and top management levels.

Given the high level heterogeneity of the sector, in terms of the institutional nature of operators, modal typologies and geographical reference areas, it may be worth looking at the following categories: local transport, mid- to long-distance transportation, infrastructures, logistics and freight transport, the environment and safety. By and large there are features common to all these categories, such as the need to consolidate the so-called horizontal competencies, knowledge of new norms, awareness of quality and service management, knowledge of ICT, etc. (Ministero dei Trasporti e della Navigazione, 2000).

These training needs are specified according to the various categories, thus giving rise to new professional figures in public and private institutions. An initial effort should be made to identify and describe such figures with a certain degree of precision, placing them on specific training programmes with focused priorities, content and operational modalities (Ministero dei Trasporti e della Navigazione, 2000).

Insofar as transport in Europe is concerned, administrative knowledge is losing importance with the abolition of customs barriers, while knowledge of integrated logistics, ICT and marketing is progressively gaining importance. The specialised skills training of personnel for the management of companies' logistics systems must therefore include thorough re-examination of the cultural parameters that have so far been used to interpret the phenomena of freight transport. Indeed, transport-related knowledge has tended, over time, to be of a predominantly bureaucratic and administrative nature and to overlook socio-economic methods of analysis (Bologna, 1992). With deregulation, all forms of training need to modernise the criteria for transport analysis and, in the light of modern industrial processes, must abandon bureaucratic approaches.

Notes

1   The most important logistics district in Europe is in Venlo, Netherlands, close to the borders with Germany and Belgium, where some of the major Japanese and American multinational companies have located their stock and distribution sites.

2   These solutions are based on the following principles: warehouses and procurements enjoy high economies of scale, in that the more these activities are shared the more benefits are gained by firms in terms of technical efficiency. The advantages of shared purchasing are greater market visibility, lower administrative costs and lower inventory management costs which, service levels being equal, are directly in proportion to the number of warehouses.

3   With reference to business-to-business, the possibility of price comparison in raw materials procurements on world markets via the Internet determines higher demand for logistics services at an international level. On the other hand, in business-to-consumer the problem is that of guaranteeing final delivery of goods generated by numerous single transactions and, at the same time, ensuring adequate service levels to extremely fragmented and diversified consignees.

4   The most significant laws are: law 84/94 on port reorganisation, favouring terminal privatisation; law 240/90 on the establishment of interports and the 'Piano Generale dei Trasporti e della Logistica 2000.'

References

Bolgna, S. (1992), 'Sui modi nuovi di muovere le merci', *Politica ed Economia*, no. 9, pp. 22-26.

Bowersox, D.J. (1990), 'The strategic benefits of logistics alliances', *Harvard Business Review*, Vol. 68, no. 4, pp. 36-45.

Carrara, M., Monticelli, M. (ed.) (1998), *Prospettive del trasporto merci a medio e lungo termine in Italia*, Centro Studi sui Sistemi di Trasporto, Turin, Italy.

Christopher, M. (1992), *Logistics and supply chain management: strategies for reducing costs and improving services*, Pitman Publishing, London.

Cooper, M.C., Lambert, D.M., Pagh, J.D. (1998), 'What should be the transportation provider's role in supply chain management ?', *8th World Conference on Transport Research*, 12-17 July, Antwerpen, Belgium.

de Langen, P.W. (1999), 'Time centrality in transport', *International Journal of Maritime Economics*, Vol. I, no. 2, October-December, pp. 41-55.

Evangelista P., Morvillo A. (2000), 'Maritime transport in the Italian logistics market,' *Maritime Policy & Management*, Vol. 27, no. 4, pp. 335-352.

Federtrasporto, (2001), 'L'internazionalizzazione del trasporto: la posizione dell'impresa italiana', *Scenari dei Trasporti*, no. 4, Rome, Italy.

Ferrozzi, C., Shapiro, R., Heskett, J. (1985), *Logistics strategy. Cases and concepts*, West Publishing Co., St. Paul, Minnesota, USA.

Gentry, J.J. (1993), 'Strategic alliances in purchasing: transportation is the vital link', *International Journal of Purchasing and Material Management*, Summer, pp. 11-16.

McKinnon, A. (1999), 'The outsourcing of logistical activities', Waters D. (edited by), *Global Logistics and Distribution Planning*, Kogan Page, London, UK.

Ministero Dei Trasporti E Della Navigazione, (2000), *Piano generale dei trasporti*, Servizio Pianificazione e Programmazione, Rome, Italy.

Morvillo, A. (2000), 'Internationalisation of the Italian shipping industry and logistics services', proceedings of the IAME (International Association of Maritime Economists) 2000 Conference *'The Maritime Industry into the Millennium: The Interaction of Theory and Practice'*, 13-15 September, Istituto Universitario Navale, Naples, Italy.

Schary, P.B., Larsen, T.S. (1995), *Managing the global supply chain*, Handelshojskolens Forlag, Copenhagen, Denmark.

Stevens, G.C. (1989), 'Integrating the supply chain', *International Journal of Physical Distribution and Materials Management*, Vol. 19, no. 8, pp. 3-8.

Chapter 2

Information and Communication Technologies: a Key Factor in Freight Transport and Logistics

Pietro Evangelista

Introduction

Information and Communication Technologies – ICT[1] – has in the last decade undergone rapid progress largely due to numerous technological developments in computer production (for example exponential increase in computer power) and in telecommunications (for example shift from analog to digital conversion, emergence of optical fibre transmission systems). These developments have assigned to ICT the undeniable role of catalyst in changing business models, relationships between firms and market structures. The literature, in turn, has devoted increasing attention to the effects of such technologies on manufacturing (for example automotive) and service industries (for example retail distribution, banking and financial services, and so on). However, less attention has been given in the past to the impact of ICT on the transport and logistics industry.

More recently, in line with the widespread use of the Internet and electronic commerce, the literature and business practice have shown a renewed interest in the effect of these technologies on the sector, owing to the higher level of complexity in logistics and transport, together with improved efficiency gains in these services through the use of ICT. In other words, the globalised sourcing of parts and components and distribution of products has highlighted the role of information in industrial processing and, at the same time, has raised the level of information intensity in transport and logistics activities. As a result, growth in the volume of electronic communication along the supply chain is expected to double by 2005 (Trilog, 1999). For example, electronic exchanges of transport documentation, invoices, order instructions and payments are forecast to grow by 59%. All of this has induced some authors to use the term 'virtual logistics' (Clarke, 1998; Crowley, 1998) intended not only as the massive use of ICT in transport and logistics services, but also as the ability of such technologies to break down the traditional barriers between firms with a view to facilitating integrated and, hence, efficient management of the supply chain.

Finally, ICT developments will influence the logistics and transport services market, shift it from a physical to an electronic one and give rise to new organisational forms for these services. To this end, a recent study conducted by

OECD (1999) has revealed how e-commerce can have differentiated effects on business models. In some cases these effects are radical and may imply revolutionary changes in a firm's management (useful examples may be found in the audio-video, publishing and retail banking sectors). In other cases e-commerce has only in part replaced traditional business models, as in the case of transport and logistics where the service providers continue to operate a large part of their business through physical forwarding and delivery infrastructure, in other words its proprietary network.

The above picture underlines the difficulties in identifying all the factors and processes involved and, furthermore, in examining their effects. If the dynamic nature of these processes is considered, along with the variety, complexity and speed of ICT systems and application changes, such difficulties will become even greater.

Unlike other industrialised countries, the Italian logistics and transport industry lags behind somewhat in adopting ICT. Generally speaking, this situation is attributed to the following factors: traditional resistance by entrepreneurs to change; small size of service providers inhibiting investment in ICT; lack of user-friendly applications; widespread use of proprietary ICT systems; finally, the inadequate ICT skills of company personnel. This last point is critical because the growing dissemination of such technologies in transport and logistics providers is making even more urgent the need for the development of new technical competencies in the use of hardware and software, the acquisition of new skills to *surf* and obtain information from hypertextual communication structures, and the know-how required in the design of communication, training and work processes.

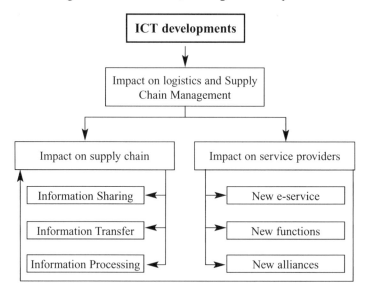

Figure 2.1 The impact of ICT on freight transport and logistics: a framework

The main aim of this chapter is to outline the impact of ICT on advanced logistics and supply chain management. Indeed, Figure 2.1 describes two clearly distinguished relationships between the impact on the supply chain and the effects on service providers, discussed in the second section.

A further objective is to discuss the degree of ICT adoption in the Italian logistics and transport industry. In the third section a brief picture of the position of Italy in the international ICT industry is given, while, in the fourth, the use of ICT in the Italian logistics and transport industry is presented. In the concluding section, policy implications in training and new professional skills development are drawn.

The Effects of ICT on Logistics and Supply Chain Management

One of the chief areas of interest that has emerged in recent years concerns the effects of new information and communication technologies applied to logistics and SCM.[2] Information systems applications in the field of supply chain management is not new and has a long history, pre-dating the use of computer power. An early example was the maintenance of inventory records on ledger cards which at first were manually updated and later became semi-mechanically updated using magnetically encoded data. As such, the computer has facilitated faster data processing and allowed significantly more data and information to be handled.[3]

Since then logistics and SCM have changed rapidly, to the extent that the relationship between ICT and the supply chain now appears to be so close that it has even become difficult to establish whether information technology is a driving force or is simply an enabling technology. What is more, in certain respects, a parallel development may be seen between the evolution of logistics and innovations in ICT. Figure 2.2 illustrates the timeline of the main applications in logistics and SCM since their introduction in the 1960s, when Electronic Data Interchange (EDI)[4] systems were first used to support logistics activity.

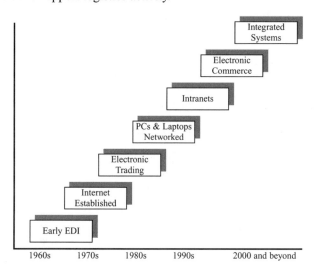

Figure 2.2 Indicative timeline of ICT applications in Supply Chain Management

There has been a plethora of works in the recent literature which, from time to time, have underlined the general aspects (Introna, 1993; Hammant, 1995) and specific effects (Peel, 1995; Kia *et al.*, 2000) of these technologies in logistics and SCM. As it is difficult to examine all their possible effects in this chapter, attention is focused only on the contribution made by ICT to the improvement of the overall efficiency in the logistics chain, through their greater integration and the effects on transport and logistics service providers.

ICT: a Tool for the Improvement of Efficiency in the Supply Chain

In the literature on SCM, both academics and managers have emphasised the role of ICT as a key integration element. ICT are meant to pervade the whole supply chain, enabling not only the integration of functions and processes of a single company, but also those of suppliers and customers with broad and long-term implications for an organisation's competitive advantage. Christopher (1997) has stated that '…organis-ations in the chain seek to create additional customer value through the exchange of information. Value is created by the management of two main flows within the supply chain, namely the flow of information and the flow of materials and goods.'

To this end, Pontrandolfo and Scozzi (1999) have recognised that in a supply chain the exchange of information frequently precedes the physical movement of materials and products. This, in turn, enables firms to reduce inventories, making material flows more effective and more efficient. Furthermore, Crowley (1998) has noted that due to developments in ICT, today it is easier to replace inventory with information, since information is becoming increasingly cheap and inventory is becoming increasingly costly. Through EDI, for instance, the inventory/information trade-off along the supply chain may be optimised.

Table 2.1 Classification of ICT applications for SCM

Function	Activity	ICT technology
Production and sharing of data and information	Access and use of data and information by supply chain partners	• Databases • Datawarehouse
Information transfer	Communication of information between supply chain partners	• EDI • E-mail • GroupWare • Internet/WEB
Information processing and utilisation	Data and e-document processing in decision making and operations planning of the supply chain	• Advanced AI • CAD • CAE • ERP • MRP • Multi-media • Traditional AI

Source: adapted from Pontrandolfo, Scozzi (1999)

The main effects of ICT on the supply chain may be analysed with reference to three functions related to information management: production and sharing of data and information, their transfer and, lastly, the processing and utilisation of information for operations planning of the supply chain (Broens et al., 1999). The specific technologies used as a support tool for the three functions identified above are summarised in Table 2.1.

Information sharing is an essential prerequisite for securing information accessibility to all supply chain partners involved in logistics operations. The creation of distributed databases fosters the development of relationships with other operators in the supply chain. In addition, the availability of consistent information improves decision-making processes for operators. This is apparent in all industrial sectors with a high level of component and parts suppliers, particularly in the aerospace and automotive industries.

Data sharing has always been important in the transport and logistics industry. Access to and availability of information in intermodal transport, for instance, contribute to substantially reducing time in freight transfer from one mode of transport to another and errors in drawing up freight documentation, thereby increasing overall transport efficiency. It must be noted, however, that information sharing may not always be easily achieved. Although recent ICT developments have mainly addressed data and information sharing both within firms and in supply chain, the dissemination of distributed databases has been hindered by the insufficient compatibility of information systems used by different supply chain partners (external barrier), and by poor integration between departments inside the firm (internal barrier).

Information transfer is another field of application to have been substantially affected by ICT developments, in that it is probably the most relevant function in the SCM concept. For example, the dispatch of a customer's order generally marks the beginning of supply chain operations, requiring the use of communication technology which, in turn, facilitates information transfer. This information transfer may take place through a variety of technology ranging from the most recent e-commerce applications or extranet, EDI systems, to the most traditional communication technology such as the telephone, telex or fax. Prior to Internet applications, the technology perhaps most investigated in SCM literature was EDI. Apart from its benefits, many authors have noted how efficient use of EDI has been constrained by the absence of user-friendly applications, poor flexibility in data transformation[5] and, finally, by the lack of widespread cross-sectoral standards, such as UN/EDIFACT (United Nations EDI for administration, commerce and transport). This has led to the creation of separate EDI standards for different sectors, such as ODETTE for the automotive industry and DISH for the shipping industry.

More recently, with the arrival of Internet and e-commerce technologies, the problem of systems and applications interoperability has to a large extent been overcome, thus extending the potential use of these technologies, including EDI, even to smaller enterprises. In using the Internet, these enterprises are no longer forced to make massive investments in order to implement such systems. Indeed, Internet technology gives rise to low-cost implementation, flexibility in data and information transfer applications through the web (e-mail, GroupWare, EDI). Moreover, they can ensure acceptable security levels guaranteed by cryptographic systems, and the separation between 'private' and 'public' access areas to web sites. In this respect, the Internet is the means by which firms will increasingly exchange information and manage supply and customer networks.

Insofar as the effects of ICT on *supply chain operations planning* is concerned, it is worth pointing out how SCM logic has given rise to a gradual yet continuous change in business processes. Whilst internal processes influenced company strategies until the end of the '80s, today exogenous factors principally affect the organisational and management decisions of companies.

The advantages stemming from better information transfer and sharing, together with greater transport efficiency in the movement of goods, have been fully recognised and appreciated and have induced many companies to reconsider the complex configuration of their supply chain activities.

ICT plays a major role in these developments, with particular reference to supply chain operations planning. Indeed, the benefits obtained from the applications of SCM logic depend almost entirely on the company's capability to establish telematic links with customers, suppliers and transport and logistics service providers to automate the highest number of supply chain operations possible.

In line with these developments, ICT investments made by firms have progressively favoured systems linking actors in the supply chain (extended supply chain focus) as opposed to setting up platforms capable of satisfying in the main the needs of single firms (internal focus).[6]

Indeed many firms, especially large sized, have concentrated investment on applied solutions which endorse the transfer from the phase of Enterprise Resources Planning[7] (ERP) applications to the phase where new applications are used to integrate all the stages of the chain, and to support the entire planning process of the extended supply chain as, for example, the new Enterprise Integration Application (EIA).[8]

These new applications are able to integrate suppliers, distributors and transport and logistics service providers. Furthermore, through these systems companies are able to combine and align their planning with that of other supply chain partners. In particular, the Advanced Planning System (APS) covers the whole area of supply chain operations, finds and makes information available in real time at any stage in the chain, and so makes the planning process more efficient. Internet technology gives support to this new concept of the extended enterprise and, to a large extent, solves communication problems between the actors involved. These systems, therefore, are capable of optimising the potential of Internet technologies used not only for business transactions (procurement and sales processes), but also to manage collaborative relations with other partners and, hence, to steer the entire supply chain. Intel, Cisco and Dell are well-known examples of firms that use the Internet to manage their supply chain. In the express courier service sector, companies such as Federal Express, UPS and DHL actively use the Internet, together with tracking and tracing applications, so as to provide their customers with information on shipment status.

It should be pointed out that the shift from the more traditional ERP systems to new systems capable of managing the entire logistics chain seems far from being in place. Indeed, it must be borne in mind that many firms, having already committed substantial resources to ICT investment (especially in ERP systems), are unwilling to start up new investment projects in more advanced applications such as EIA. For many firms, integrating with legacy systems is a further problem not to be overlooked. These systems continue to form the most important part of a company's information systems, since they contain the most critical applications and company data. In the majority of cases, this legacy systems are not integrated with recent e-business applications because the problems of integration are considerably complex.

Due to these factors, many firms are reluctant to venture into the field of ICT investments at a cross-organisational level and, consequently, give little importance to investment in the whole logistics chain. In fact, many supply chain management initiatives are not oriented to integrating the entire logistics chain, but are focused on co-ordinating small groups of firms (two or three at the most). These observations are largely confirmed by a recent study conducted on a sample of leading European companies in some industrial and service sectors (Edwards, Peters and Sharman, 2001). The investigation revealed a low level of supply chain integration and an equally low level of information system integration. Only a few companies declared that they had implemented ERP systems which, nonetheless, had not been used to integrate the whole business process. Moreover, in none of the firms interviewed had EIA systems been implemented to support links with trading partners, while most of the firms still use EDI in commercial information transfer.

The Impact of ICT on Transport and Logistics Service Providers

Examination of the impact of ICT on the operations planning of the supply chain has highlighted the fact that such technologies have become a determining factor for each firm intending to manage an integrated supply chain. For manufacturers and retailers, information management has therefore become as critical as the physical movement of goods. As a result, poor ICT resource management by one or more actors in the supply chain could have negative repercussions on the performance of the entire logistics chain in terms of costs, planning ability and customer service (Lee and Billington, 1992). In other words, measures adopted to improve overall efficiency of the chain may be compromised by the inappropriate use of ICT by an actor operating in a different stage of the chain. Thus, in this respect the choice of logistics provider has strategic value,[9] one of the selection criteria being the provider's information technology capabilities.[10] From here stems the pressing demand by manufacturers and retailers for all actors in the chain to place even more attention on integrating their business systems through ICT and Internet technologies. Evidence of this lies in the increasing adoption by these firms of software for the integrated management of their supply chain operations.

It is obvious that, under this strong pressure, transport and logistics service providers have attached growing importance to ICT in the management of their business. Integration and co-ordination with other actors in the supply chain, and especially with other logistics and transport service providers, have become vital elements in the business strategies of such firms.

These developments raise two important questions: What are the effects of ICT on transport and logistics service providers? How are ICT and the Internet changing the business model of such firms and what are the effects on strategic decisions? The answer to these questions is not straightforward, above all because the dissemination of Internet-linked technologies in these firms is so recent as to make the analysis of their impact difficult. Nevertheless, some effects appear to be emerging and are briefly described as follows.

New e-services – One of the first visible effects is the integration of traditional services with 'new information services' spurred by the dissemination of the Internet. Although transport firms have used telecommunication systems and networks for some time,[11] the sector as a whole may not be considered a leader in the field of technological innovation (Tilanus, 1997). However, over the last few years firms operating in the sector have made significant progress in their adoption of new technologies, particularly those linked to the Internet and e-commerce. Low-cost access to the Web and the dissemination of e-commerce technologies have provided these firms with the tool to satisfy customer demand by using traditional services in conjunction with growing information-based services. Today, the main transport and logistics service firms are in a position to provide a variety of information via the Internet[12] and to secure transactions online with customers. However, the range of initiatives online appears to be somewhat diversified.

There are firms that initially used their own web sites as electronic service catalogues. Some firms have started to offer rudimentary tracking and booking services, while others have tried to create a competitive advantage with their web pages by developing signature options unique to their brands. For example, the shipping company OOCL has developed a means to release bills of lading over the Internet. In other cases customised portals have been developed to provide support capabilities that can also be tailored to languages other than English. APL is a good example of these advanced applications of Internet portals.[13] However, the rapid development of e-commerce is expected to give rise to a gradual increase in functionality to web sites.

Despite such developments, problems still occur when transport and logistics firms make use of e-commerce solutions. One of the most frequent problems is in shipment tracking and tracing. As each shipment often involves more than one carrier, a shipper wishing to track a single shipment has to consult the Web pages of each logistics provider involved in the shipment. The tracking of several shipments thus involves moving between different company web sites, with obvious time wastage and uncertain outcomes. Similar problems recur when a shipper has to find a provider to forward a single shipment. In this latter case, the shipper also has to visit the Internet sites of various transport service providers for price and service details in order to compare and choose the provider who best satisfies his needs. Such an approach clearly has its limits. First, the Web search may prove difficult to carry out or, at any rate, may not guarantee satisfactory results. In addition, the selection of provider tends to be largely based on price rather than on the service quality. Finally, the shipper might contact and use providers who are new to him and whose reliability and performance in service is unknown.

New functions – The above problems originate from the fact that in such a large market as transport and logistics, there is so much information that the operators in the supply chain find it difficult at times to locate the information being sought, or to simply manage the information available to them. This has opened up new opportunities for the development of new roles and functions in the supply chain, i.e.

information brokers, or infomediaries. The purpose of these web-based intermediaries is to give added value to the transport and logistics business through greater efficiency and information transparency. Their work is based on running web sites – Internet transport portals – which bring together buyers and sellers of transport services, provide the buyer with information and make communication between the two faster and more direct. As for their services, whilst on the one hand there is a strong similarity between the services of different portals, on the other hand there are significant differences in the scope and objectives of these portals (UNCTAD, 2000). There is also a variety of infomediary typologies operating on the Internet. Even though it may not be possible to give a comprehensive taxonomy of such typologies, due to the extremely dynamic nature of the sector, a recent study by Regan and Song (2001) has identified at least five different categories: Spot Freight Markets, Auction and Request for Quote (RFQ) markets, Exchanges, Applications Service Providers (ASPs) and Purchasing Consolidation Markets.[14]

The authors add that the dividing lines between the first four typologies are somewhat blurred. Some Exchanges are typically ASPs or teamed with ASPs. Exchanges also offer spot market and auction services. Some examples are 3PLEX, Nistevo, Leanlogistics and Trantislink. Logistics.com and Celarix, leaders in the auction and RFQ space, appear to be ASPs more than freight marketplaces. They will face stiff competition from companies previously in the off-line logistics solutions business like I2 and Manugistics and from new logistics ASPs like Accuship. Another interesting case of ASP includes those companies providing web-enabling technology to handle the package and LTL shipments generated by e-commerce companies. Examples of these are GoShip and Intershipper. These work with a large number of couriers and develop solutions for clients who ship large or small volumes of packages each day. These companies compete directly with UPS and FedEx who provide similar web solutions for e-commerce companies.

Accordingly, the spread of infomediaries tends to alter the role of traditional transport intermediaries and relations between these firms and other actors in the logistics chain. There is little doubt that development of the Internet and e-commerce have led to far more information being made available to all actors along the supply chain. This may pose a threat to operators such as agents and freight forwarders, who have based their business on information asymmetries between operators requiring and others providing transport and logistics services. Some intermediary functions risk becoming redundant, to be subsequently replaced by the phenomenon of disintermediation.[15] The pressure of this threat has induced some intermediaries to form alliances with other transport operators, as in the case of the recent alliance between AEI, a freight forwarder company, and the shipping line P&O. They have set-up a strategic alliance to send standard EDI shipping instructions and bookings and receive tracking information in return.

From a different point of view, the development of infomediaries may provide traditional intermediaries with a good opportunity to extend and differentiate their own business. Indeed in many cases, web sites are accessed by carriers, shippers and intermediaries. There are also some web sites entirely devoted to the transport intermediaries and shippers they serve. The services provided via these web sites tend to improve rather than threaten the role of intermediaries. Freight forwarders, for example, may become truly global multimodal and logistics service providers, focusing on the entire chain process rather than on the narrow region of origin or destination under the traditional approach. Consequently their key competencies are shifting from traditional agency-based freight forwarding services (for example freight documentation, customs clearance) to optimising the total transport and logistics needs of shippers. In the maritime transport industry, a similar process is affecting shipping agents and NVOCCs. From this standpoint, it may be concluded that emerging Internet-based transport services are able to provide traditional intermediaries with a tool for improving their efficiency and accessing new customers and new market segments. Use of the Internet by these firms could even be a means of entering into direct competition with the carriers themselves, as in the case of BDP International, a logistics company with great emphasis on information technology. Such a company has created an NVOCC subsidiary that can take out block bookings of container slots on ships. Once it has taken out such a block booking, which is negotiated at a favourable rate, BDP is free to sell the slots on to its own customers. BDP will also handle all of the administrative issues involved in the process in a more efficient manner as BDP is in possession of highly advanced ICT competencies and tools. Operating in this way, BDP is pushing ocean carriers into a commodity position of doing nothing more than owning, managing and operating the vessels as BDP handles all administrative, marketing and management issues.

The considerations and examples reported above point out the degree of dissemination and use of infomediaries. It is very difficult to carry out an empirical study on the real impact of web transport portals, since there is little consistent data on the overall volume of services sold via portals. This problem is unlikely to be resolved until carriers remove confidentiality constraints on their service rates. These firms, in fact, seem reluctant to use infomediaries since they would be forced to share confidential information which, once disclosed, could be used to gain control of customer relations through, for example, management of the booking process and the rate charged. Actually, a small number of traditional intermediaries are using online exchanges to help their shipper clients match with carriers. One inhibiting factor is the lack of technical personnel with Internet and e-commerce skills.

A recent study carried out by the consulting firm KPMG and the market research company, Benchmarking Partners, on the way in which carriers use Internet (Logistics Management & Distribution Report, 2000) would appear to confirm the above findings. The study consisted in monitoring a sample of 22 of the main carriers, 14 manufacturers and retailers, and 8 financial analysts. The findings suggest that over the next two years transport service providers will concentrate increasingly on web-based transactions, such as online ordering, tracking and tracing shipments, rather than Internet-based strategic activities, such as joint planning of the supply chain.

In answer to the question concerning their plans to invest in the Internet, transport providers stated that the aim of such investment was to focus more on lowering costs than on improving customer service which, in their view, was adequate. Despite the efforts of transport carriers, shippers, claim that a lot remains to be done as far as customer relations are concerned. The shippers also declared that tracking and tracing, customer self-help capabilities and transparency of the shipment for all the other supply chain partners make up the principal Internet-based capabilities that they require from transport provider. As for their actual involvement in e-commerce, only 38% of the carriers interviewed claimed to have assigned to a manager the task of supervising e-commerce as a separate business activity. A further interesting finding concerns the limited role played by so-called transportation infomediaries. About 50% of the shippers interviewed replied that they might use infomediaries in the near future, while carriers do not foresee that infomediaries will have a significant effect on their business.

New alliances – Another feature emerging alongside the Internet and e-commerce development is the creation of a new category of service provider called Fourth Party Logistics Provider (4PL). According to Bade et al. (1999), Fourth-Party Logistics Provider is a supply chain integrator who assembles and manages the resources, capabilities and technology of its organisation with those of complementary service providers to deliver a comprehensive supply chain solution. In brief, the emergence of these providers derives from the fact that many manufacturers and retailers operating at an international level find it increasingly difficult to satisfy the growing expectations of their customers, mainly because of the widespread use of the Internet and Web-based solutions and that of enterprise integration technologies. Pressures from customers are therefore forcing these firms to reassess their supply chain strategies, especially in terms of strategy, operations and technology. The traditional response has been the outsourcing of a growing part of their transport and logistics activity to Third Party Logistics providers, so as not to commit additional investment resources to buying in technology and professional skills. Nevertheless, this option is proving to be limited, especially in consideration of the fact that, as already shown, these providers do not yet possess all the skills (above all technological and strategic) required to satisfy the demands of the customer. In order to improve their skills, some transport and logistics providers have started to secure alliances with complementary service providers (Rockwell, 1999). Some of these alliances have been formed with management consulting companies and technology providers, as in the case of Ryder Integrated Logistics and its alliance with IBM, Accenture, i2 Technologies and SeeBeyond. In this alliance, IBM operates Ryder's systems and customer call centres and works directly with Ryder on specific technology projects and SeeBeyond, a leader in Web-based integration technology, helps Ryder proactively manage by exception, solving a problem before it can impact a customer. The emergence of Fourth Party Logistics Providers enables manufacturers to outsource to a single organisation the entire re-engineering of their supply chain processes, beginning with the design stage through to implementation, and ending with the execution of comprehensive supply chain solutions. In technological terms, solutions provided by 4PL help to achieve technological uniformity deriving from the exploitation of the management consultants' technological capabilities as well as that of the transport and logistics service providers.

Beyond the emerging figure of the Fourth Party Logistics Provider, there is an ongoing trend in the transport and logistics service sector to form alliances with other firms operating in complementary sectors, as is demonstrated by the following cases and the data in Table 2.2 (cf. Eyefortransport, 2001, pp. 56-65).

Table 2.2 Supply-chain technology related acquisitions

Aquired Company	Aquirer	Date	Service Provided
I-ship	Stamps.com	11/01/99	web-based aggregator
Rockport Trade Systems	QRS Corp.	02/01/00	ITL services
E-Transport	Descartes Systems	02/01/00	ocean transport exchange
HomeRuns.com	Cypress Group	02/14/00	B2C e-fulfillment
eraterequest.com	Neomodal.com	03/01/00	ocean freight exchange
Infinity logistics/Automated logistics	E-Stamp	05/25/00	logistics software
QuoteShip.com	Logistics.com	06/28/00	ocean/air cargo exchange
Interface Systems	Tumbleweed	06/29/00	securee-mail
Kewill (logistics division)	Swisslog	07/17/00	WMS
Disticom Systems	Tecsys	07/19/00	shipping automation
US Certified Letters, LLC	Nextpath	07/31/00	secure e-mail
Isreal Commerce Community Ltd	Elbit Ltd.	08/09/00	web logistics
Ford customs operations	Vastera	07/14/00	import-export operations
BCE Emergis unit	Descartes Systems	12/21/00	network messaging
Intrepa	Manhattan Associates	10/24/00	TMS
AllPoints Systems	EXE Technologies	01/19/01	WMS
Agile	Ariba	01/29/01	Collaboration

Source: Bear, Stearns & Co. Inc., 2001

The parcel delivery company Federal Express has developed an 'integration bridge' that connects FedEx's PowerShip software directly into the SAP R/3 ERP system. With that connection, any R/3 user can get FedEx tracking information within R/3. ERP systems are designed primarily to streamline and automate a company's business planning processes.

UPS is developing tools that allow shippers to build end-to-end shipping features, including tracking information, into their web sites and e-marketplaces. UPS recently announced an alliance with i2 Technologies, a provider of supply-chain management and e-marketplace solutions. UPS is also working on projects with Open Market, PeopleSoft and IBM. The UPS alliance with Open Market is developing a software component known as an application-programming interface (API) that will allow Open Market's Transact enterprise software to trade information with the UPS tracking system. Transact will be able to generate a ship order directly to UPS and UPS, in turn, will automatically convey the tracking number back to Transact without the necessity of re-keying data. In the case of IBM, UPS is also working on a product called UPS Online Professional to create a customised system for international shipping that will generate 36 different kinds of customised reports. UPS has also completed a collaboration with the software developer iCat Corporation which allows online retailers to update their web sites with a UPS shipping component. The plug-in product enables web site retailers to calculate automatically UPS shipping costs for customer purchases according to shipment weight, destination, and service option.

The Position of Italy in the International ICT Market

The considerations in the second section highlight the close relationship between ICT and the transport and logistics service industry. The literature referred to and the cases presented show that the development of the transport and logistics service sector and its future structure can no longer be considered separately from innovations in the ICT sector. This means that development and efficiency of a country's transport and logistics service industry will depend more so on its position in the international technological scenario.

In this scenario it is well known that Italy lags behind. All the indicators related to the market, product dissemination and industrial production, rank Italy below the position of most European countries, Japan and USA. According to the Assinform report (2001), in the year 2000 around 48 million PCs were sold in the United States, followed by the nearest rival Japan (38 million), and then the main European countries: Germany (23 million), United Kingdom (20 million) and France (approx. 15 million). With its 9 million PCs, Italy lies very much behind. Further, the comparison of IT expenditure between different macro areas leads to similar results. The United States shows the highest pro-capita IT expenditure (US$ 1,298), while Italy and Spain come much further down with US$ 371 and US$ 258 respectively. Likewise, in the United States the IT share of GDP is 4.1%, about 3% in Japan, United Kingdom, Germany and France, whereas in Italy it stands at 1.7%.

Despite this gap, some signs of an inverse trend emerged in 2000, proving how ICT plays an increasingly strategic role in Italy's economy. Investment trends in IT showed a more dynamic performance amounting to 19.4% compared with total investments in the Italian ICT sector.

2000 was a particularly good year for IT, with faster growth than in 1999, and a rate of growth which, for the first time in many years, exceeded that of all other major European countries except Spain.[16] In 2000 Italy once again achieved double-digit growth: the market reached a value of Itl 36,710 bn, as against Itl 32,608 bn the previous year, an increase of 12.6%.

The adoption of ICT in Italy is still predominantly concentrated in large and medium sized enterprises, even though the demand from small companies grew in 2000.[17] A growing demand for IT comes from the manufacturing sector. Large companies are demanding e-business solutions with particular reference to Customer Relationship Management (CRM) and e-procurement, while small companies located in the industrial districts are showing increasing interest in new technologies.

Insofar as e-commerce is concerned, the survey conducted by Assinform and NetConsulting highlighted a variety of situations among leading Italian companies. Some companies (8%) have already implemented e-business solutions and have no intention of allocating further investments; others (36%) are reluctant to introduce e-commerce solutions; still others (20%) have implemented a few limited projects; finally, there are companies (36%) fully oriented towards e-business solutions in the near future.

Analysis of the e-business areas in which companies are focusing investments shows that 1999 was dedicated essentially to the creation of web sites (before portals) and Customer Relationship Management solutions. In 2000, investments in this area remained very strong, with the addition of marketing and Sales Force Automation functionality. Companies also began to invest in Marketplace creation and e-Procurement, whilst the percentage of Supply Chain Management projects was relatively small.

Finally, the Assinform analysis of investments in various business sectors showed diversification, determined by a number of variables such as competitive intensity in the sector, degree of internationalisation, average size of the firm and the degree of obsolescence in technology and applications installed. Therefore, the most dynamic sectors are precisely those engaged in international competition and that have committed massive investments in ICT, such as telecommunications, banking, insurance and commercial distribution.

ICT in the Transport and Logistics Sector in Italy

The delay on the part of Italy in adopting ICT technologies has negatively affected the efficiency of the entire transport system and, at the same time, has proved to be a constraint for the development of transport and logistics service providers. However, it should be pointed out that, besides Italy's backward position in the international technological scenario, there are other constraints contributing to the poor dissemination of ICT in the sector:

♦ low level of technological and organisational innovation in Italian transport and logistics service companies
♦ inadequate IT skills of personnel in such companies
♦ poor exposure to ICT in SMEs.

The characteristics of demand and supply of transport and logistics services in the Italian market has a significant impact on the above constraints (Evangelista, Morvillo, 2000). The effects of such factors on the developments of ICT in this market may be summarised as follows:

♦ on the demand side, the existence of cultural constraints *vis-à-vis* logistics is mainly due to the marked presence of SMEs in the manufacturing sector. This produces a low level of outsourcing of logistics activities beyond transportation;
♦ on the supply side, the small size of companies and their high number in each stage of the transport and logistics chain. Consequently, they are not able to control the entire transport and logistics process; such control has been yielded to large foreign companies.

With regard to this last point, the increasing presence of some large international foreign transport and logistics groups (Tnt, Deutche Post, Eurogate, Abx)[18] in the Italian market has been facilitated by the fragmentation of the transport and logistics service sector.

Despite the lack of data and specific surveys, it is worth noting that the above factors have played a major role in determining the low level of ICT adoption in Italian transport and logistics companies.

This has held back the development of technological and organisational innovation processes needed to compete in a market characterised by the more complex requirements of customers.

On the other hand, competitive driving forces in the international arena impose a higher level of consolidation. This has led to a growing number of both horizontal (aimed at achieving higher economies of scale) and vertical (aimed to better integrate the supply chain beyond the transport phase) alliances, mergers and acquisitions. Good examples may be easily found in the liner shipping industry (Evangelista, Morvillo, 1999; Evangelista, *et al.*, 2001) as well as in the port terminal sector (Heaver, *et al.*, 2000).

This process has been widely accompanied by a gradual but continued sharing of companies' information systems and technology. The largest groups and major companies are directing their efforts to improving communication between partners in the supply chain. The growing use of standards for information transfer together with greater collaboration among partners in the chain demonstrate that there are encouraging signs of genuine understanding of the benefits to be accrued from ICT. The creation of community-based ICT services, such as the new portals being introduced collaboratively to fully exploit the potential of the Internet and e-commerce in the liner shipping industry,[19] is a relevant example (Evangelista, Stumm, 2000).

In Italy, on the other hand, the trends and initiatives achieved in the field of information systems and ICT for the transport and logistics sector have been characterised by a marked delay. Indeed, the process of consolidation has developed at a far slower pace than in other countries. This has inevitably had repercussions on the willingness of firms to adopt new technologies which, nonetheless, remain at a substantially low level. With regard to firms in the sector, two different profiles appear to co-exist. The first encompasses the many small and even smaller firms which operate chiefly at a local level, direct their efforts on their organisational agility, pricing and thus cost reduction, utilise IT mainly for accounting and administration processes, possess traditional ICT equipment based on the telephone, fax and telex, yet few of them have telematic links with other operators in the chain.

The second profile refers to larger firms which only recently have begun to develop links with customers and providers. Nevertheless, the systems used by these firms are chiefly 'proprietary', thus enabling automated data and information to be exchanged with a limited number of other operators. It is precisely in these firms that EDI and the Internet are used as tools to speed up physical and information flows.

These observations are largely confirmed by a survey carried out on the level of computerisation and ICT investments of transport and logistics operators in Northern Italy, specifically the Genoa-Savona area (Merlino, Testa, 1998). The survey examined 197 firms and found that they are at the initial stage of adopting ICT and that their investments in new technology are still motivated by a tactical rather than strategic logic. As for the main technology adopted by the sample firms, the survey showed a reluctance in the use of databases to share internal information with other operators. Another finding showed the growth of investment in EDI technology, but few messages were exchanged owing to the different protocols used by operators, with a consequent inflexibility in buyer-supplier relationships. Even the use of the Internet in most cases is still at a relatively early stage; indeed, only 1/5 of PCs were connected to the Web in the firms surveyed. Furthermore, the Web is hardly ever used to sell services. Most of the firms interviewed stated that the Internet was confined to collecting information, advertising and, in a few cases, to communicating with their own customers. Finally, the survey highlighted that the dissemination of new technologies is proceeding at an intermittent and non-homogeneous pace. This can be attributed in large part to the background history of the firm and its entrepreneurial culture. The latter aspect is especially important in defining the technological profile of SMEs. Another survey conducted on a sample of 48 shipping agents and freight forwarders located in Southern Italy, specifically Campania region, confirmed the above aspect (Minguzzi, Morvillo, 1999). It also found that the willingness to invest in computer hardware and software is generally motivated by personal reasons rather than economic considerations.

The results of both studies underline a contrasting picture where ICT is concerned. While on the one hand the awareness of ICT as a success factor for the firm is evident, on the other the low level of ICT adoption with particular reference to the Internet and e-commerce tools is surprising. Nonetheless, there are interesting signs of dynamism. Grimaldi, one of the leading European Ro-Ro shipping carriers of vehicles, has recently conducted a series of operations that may be defined as proactive internationalisation. They consist, firstly, in launching joint services with other foreign firms and, secondly, in assuming the direct management of terminal areas in foreign ports as Setubal in Spain, Cork in Ireland, and Esbjerg in Denmark, and Antewerpen in the Schelde region. This second operation, in particular, can be mainly attributed to a contract signed in mid-1999 between Grimaldi and Fiat. As in other logistics outsourcing contracts in the automotive industry, the agreement between Grimaldi and Fiat required the same IT systems to be shared (Drewry, 2000). As a result of this agreement, Grimaldi became responsible for the first door-to-door movement of 80,000 new Fiat, Alfa Romeo and Lancia cars from eight Italian factories to Fiat dealers in Spain. Grimaldi has therefore assumed the control of Fiat's logistics chain in Spain and the lead time for delivery of cars has been cut by up to four days.

Conclusion and Implications for Training

The analysis conducted in the preceding sections shows how ICT is exerting a substantial influence on reorganisation and integration processes of supply chains and on transport and logistics service providers as well. In these firms, new information technologies are playing a central role in redefining management and organisational processes in addition to stimulating renewal of their technology through new information and telematic infrastructures.

However, these processes of transformation are not easily achievable, nor are they without risks. Indeed, for full integration to be achieved with its partners, a firm must not only activate interfunctional processes involving customers and providers but, above all, has to address the fundamentally important human factor. As a consequence, it is the human and not the technological component that is most affected by these processes of change, precisely because the higher level of performance attained through the use of new technologies, especially the Internet and e-commerce, is inevitably linked to the strategic role of human resources and training.

These considerations are particularly critical for transport and logistics service providers. This chapter has clearly shown that these firms compete in two separate yet closely linked markets: first the marketplace, where goods are physically exchanged and where traditional transport services are required for the shipment of goods; secondly, the marketspace, in other words the virtual market of e-commerce where information is the main objective of transaction.

In terms of competencies, on the one hand these firms are required to continue to provide transport services using their traditional competencies (marketplace) and, on the other hand, this function must be integrated with the supply of information and the related development of new professional expertise in line with ICT and the Internet (marketspace).

The literature and cases described in this chapter have highlighted how the main international transport and logistics service companies are redefining their respective roles and business processes through the use of ICT. This may be demonstrated by the growing involvement in new e-services and new forms of alliance with firms supplying complementary services, such as software vendors. In large transport and logistics companies, training has become central for competencies and new professional profiles to be developed in an organic way.

The transport and logistics industry in Italy provides a different picture altogether. The marked presence of small and very small providers has led to the use of ICT largely as a support tool for administration and accounting management, whereas information and telematic links with other operators in the transport and logistics chain are limited. Only recently have providers begun to make use of telematic links, but the use of EDI and Internet tools appears to be still at an early stage. The Internet, for instance, is hardly ever used to sell services, its use being mainly limited to gathering information and advertising. Finally, for all their awareness of ICT technologies as an important factor of company success, Italian firms still lag far behind in the adoption of new technologies.

The substantial impact of foreign competition has further reduced stimulus towards innovation since it has contributed to the disappearance of medium sized providers that could have guided and disseminated innovation processes in the sector. This has produced an effect which may be defined as *technological polarisation*. In other words, in the Italian market ICT are mainly concentrated in large international groups, while small firms continue to lag behind, a situation that may lead to further marginalisation of Italian SMEs together with a total loss of control of logistics flows across the country.

What are the policy implications emerging from the above picture? There appear to be two possible directions for intervention.

Firstly, in the field of training, interventions can no longer be delayed. In order to secure a sustainable competitive edge deriving from the adoption of new technologies, small companies need to ensure that new competencies and new organisational behaviour are developed. Training is therefore a critical tool in new and existing professional profiles. Training interventions for new professional competencies have to address both specialist and technician profiles (for example

Programmers in HTML/XML, Network Engineers, Security Managers, Webmasters and System Engineers) and strategic and management profiles (for example E-business Project Managers, Content Managers, Communication Experts and Change Managers). As for existing professional competencies, training interventions should have the following characteristics: they must be available *when* and *where* they are required, accessible to all employees, immediate, effective and not costly. Training interventions should be targeted and short, to prevent staff becoming demotivated and absent too long from the workplace. It is precisely in these circumstances that Distance Learning can be of critical importance. As Distance Learning is largely carried out through online interactive courses (e-learning), it responds to the above characteristics. Finally, training in small companies should be preceded by consultancy aimed at restructuring business processes and identifying the training needs of every single professional profile.

Secondly, due to the marked presence of small and very small firms in the Italian transport and logistics sector, the role of the State is crucial in the provision of more financial resources and in ensuring interventions are maintained in the long term.

With regard to training expenditure, Italy lags behind when compared to the major European countries. Spending on training by companies is generally limited and poorly planned. It is well known that insufficient investment in training leads to the loss of business opportunities. In addition, it causes higher labour costs owing to the scarcity of skilled personnel on the market, reducing profitability and turnover. This can also be attributed to 'skills shortage' which in Italy has assumed alarming proportions.[20] For these reasons, the effects of this shortage are felt far more in SMEs than in large companies.

This phenomenon should spur the State to reassess education and training systems at all levels in order to meet the professional and skills needs of companies, thereby enabling them to evolve in line with technological innovation processes. This poses a challenge for education and training institutions, in that it will imply adjusting existing programmes and/or developing new ones to meet the new needs in executive development targeted at entry-level management positions. More specifically, these institutions should provide mixes of education and training in cross-functional knowledge and skills across and within the supply chain context, for example combining knowledge in ICT and Supply Chain Management.

Notes

1   OECD (1998) defines the ICT industry on the basis of two principles. For *manufacturing* industries, the products of a candidate industry must be intended to fulfil the function of information processing and communication including transmission and display and must use electronic processing to detect, measure and/or record physical phenomena or to control a physical process. For *services* industries, the products of a candidate industry must be intended to enable the function of information processing and communication by electronic means.

2   Arntzen *et al.* (1995) claimed that such interest is demonstrated by the growing number of companies that have designed and implemented new information systems and technologies for SCM.

3   Subsequently, as result of a number of developments such as growth in computer power,

lower unit cost of data processing, reduction in size of processors, the initial applications and systems developed into more flexible systems which automated one or more activities (for example purchase order generation, invoice reconciliation with goods received and sold and payment authorisation).

4   Hammant (1995, p. 33) defines EDI as 'the computer to computer exchange of inter- and intra-company business and technical data, based upon the use of agreed standards.'

5   The term flexibility has been used in this chapter in the sense intended by Pontradolfo e Scozzi (1999, p. 722) in other words '...the ability of ICT to handle different types of data and information in terms of codification and formats (text, tables, graphs, images, audio, video). According to this definition EDI systems are considered to be inflexible because they can only manage highly codified information.

6   McDonnell and Sweeney (2001) have set up an updated overview of the main ICT solutions supporting SCM. They proposed a taxonomy based on the distinction between *Point Solutions* which fulfil a particular function within one of the component parts of the supply chain (buy, make, move or sell) and *Enterprise Solutions* that integrate elements of the enterprise or the supply chain, linking the output of one action to other related elements.

7   ERP systems are information platforms designed to facilitate exchange and inter-organisational sharing of information and planning systems. In recent years, the ERP systems market has experienced rapid growth since their adoption in many industrial sectors. Yet only a limited number of vendors operate in this market, chief among them being SAP, Oracle, PeopleSoft, Baan and J.D. Edwards.

8   This is confirmed by forecasts relating to this service market which is likely to increase from $5,4000 million in 2000 to $20,5000 million in 2005 (SMAU Ricerche, 2001).

9   For manufacturers and retailers who sell their products through business-to-consumer e-commerce, the choice of transport and logistics service provider has an even higher strategic value. Indeed, for web transactions the delivery factor becomes an integral part of the product quality and/or the service, so making the quality and range of logistics services provided also an integral component of the company brand. Furthermore, it creates a more direct type of relationship between the logistics service provider and the end customer (Politecnico di Milano, Assologistica, 2001).

10 In relation to this, it is interesting to read the declaration made by Justin Strother, the centralised operations manager of Fleming Companies Inc. of Lewisville, Texas, USA 'When we select carriers, we not only ask about rates and services, but also their technological capabilities. Some carriers may have competitive rates, but if they don't have the technology in place, they can actually end up being more expensive. It costs us more to have to arrange for an employee to follow up and double-check on their activities.' (Atkinson, 2001).

11 The first applications were tried out in the air transport sector at the beginning of the 1960s. Later, their use was extended first to maritime transport and then, in the 1980s, to other transport modes.

12 This refers to the supply in real time of information concerning for example freight rate, booking, routing and scheduling, tracking and tracing, shipment documentation and freight billing.

13 APL's Internet and e-commerce services are among the most sophisticated of this type in the liner shipping industry. Two are the most important e-services offered by the APL's web site: HomePort, a customised homepage tailored specifically to certain customers, and QuickReport, an online service to generate automatic reports tailored to the user's specifications.

14 *Spot market*: a spot market allows shippers and carriers to post available loads or capacity on the web; *Auction and RFQ*: an auction space provides automated RFQ and auction

capability; *Exchange*: an exchange may provide spot market and auction capabilities but must also provide creative e-commerce solutions for shippers, carriers and 3PLs; *ASPs*: Application service providers are primarily developing web-enabling and e-commerce enabling technology for the logistics industry; *Purchasing consolidation sites*: these sites provide an opportunity for member companies (typically small carriers) to purchase equipment and supplies at bulk rates over the internet.

15 Stough (2001) defines the disintermediation process as '…the bypassing of intermediaries between buyer and seller by introducing a middle man.'

16 One reason for the IT market growth rate in Italy topping the average rate for the main European countries by approximately 1 percentage point and the US rate by 2 points can be seen by analysing the impact of the various growth drivers in the different countries in 2000. Essentially there were two main drivers: the demand for technology, solutions and services linked to the start-up of major e-business and e-commerce projects by large companies and organisations; the growth in demand from SMEs, self-employed professionals and consumers.

17 Due the dissemination of the Internet and e-mail, in the last three years Italian SMEs have been gradually bridging the gap in using ICT tools. In 1997, the rate of computerisation in small firms (from 5 to 19 employees) stood less than 30%, while today it is on average higher than 80%. In 2000, IT investments made by firms with less than 250 employees increased by 14.9%, which amounts to less than 9 mln Euro (17,000 bln Lira), in other words around 45% of the total market.

18 In the two-year period 1998-1999, MIT was acquired by Deutsche Post; Tecnologistica, Traco, Rinaldi, Pony Express, Spedimacc and Ase Transport were acquired by TNT Post Group, and Saima Avandero by ABX.

19 There have been two main initiatives in this respect: the first comprises five lines (P&O Nedlloyd, Maersk Sealand, Mediterranean Shipping, Hamburg-Sud and CMA CGM) that were initial members of an Internet provider of business-to-business (B2B) ocean freight services called INTTRA (Damas, 2001); in the second, nine lines (APL, CP Ships, Hanjin, Hyundai, K Line, Mitsui OSK, Senator Yang Ming and Zim) are members of the Global Transportation Network – GTN (APL, 2000).

20 According to some estimates, the 'skills shortage' in Italy will produce a reduction in GNP of about 17,000 billion Lira in 2001, in other words approx 0.85% of GNP (Assinform, 2001).

References

APL – American President Line (2000), APL Press release, Dec. 4, www.apl.com/

Arntzen, B.C., Brown, G.C., Harrison, T.P., Trafton, L.L. (1995), 'Global supply chain at Digital Equipment Corporation', *Interfaces*, 25, (1), pp. 69-63.

Assinform (2001), Rapporto sull'informatica e le telecomunicazioni, Milan, Italy.

Atkinson, W. (2001), 'How E-Logistics Changes Shipper-Carrier Relationships', *Logistics Management & Distribution Report*, The state of E-logistics, April, http://www.manufacturing.net

Bade, D., Mueller, J. and Youd, B. (1999), *Technology in the next level of supply chain outsourcing. Leveraging the capabilities of Fourth Party Logistics*, http://bade.ascet.com

Bear, Stearns & Co. Inc. (2001), *Supply-Chain Technology*, http://www.bearstearns.com

Broens, D.F., Vanroye, K., Demkes, R. (1999), 'E-commerce, supply chain management and intermodality', background paper for the *3rd EU-USA Forum on Freight Intermodalism*, Boston, USA.

Christopher, M. (1997) *Marketing Logistics*, p. 77, Butterworth-Heinemann, Oxford.

Clarke, P.M. (1998), 'Virtual logistics. An introduction and overview of the concepts', *International Journal of Physical Distribution & Logistics Management*, Vol. 28 no. 7, pp. 486-507.

Crowley, A.G. (1998), 'Virtual logistics: transport in the marketspace', *International Journal of Physical Distribution & Logistics Management*, Vol. 28 no. 7, pp. 547-574.

Damas, P. (2001), 'INTTRA states its case', *American Shipper*, Vol. 43 no. 3, pp.61-63.

Drewry (2000), *I.T. and Shipping: new technology and new thinking leading to commercial advantage*, Drewry Shipping Consultants Ltd., January, London, UK.

Edwards, P., Peters, M., Sharman, G. (2001), 'The effectiveness of information systems in supporting the extended supply chain', *Journal of Business Logistics*, Vol. 22 no. 1, pp. 1-27.

Evangelista, P., Heaver, T., Morvillo, A. (2001), 'Liner shipping strategies for supply chain management', proceedings of the 9th *World Conference on Transport Research*, Seoul, South Korea.

Evangelista, P., Morvillo, A. (2000), 'Maritime transport in the Italian logistics market', *Maritime Policy & Management*, Vol. 27 no. 4, pp. 335-352.

Evangelista, P., Morvillo, A. (1999), 'Alliances in liner shipping: an instrument to gain operational efficiency or supply chain integration?', *International Journal of Logistics: Research and Applications*, Vol. 2 no. 1, pp. 21-38.

Evangelista, P., Stumm, M. (2000), 'Information technology issues in maritime transport: how to better integrate liner shipping in the supply chain', proceedings of the IAME (International Association of Maritime Economists) 2000 Conference *The Maritime Industry into the Millennium: The Interaction of Theory and Practice*, 13-15 September, Istituto Universitario Navale, Naples, Italy.

Eyefortransport (2001), *Digital Logistics – Value Creation in the Freight Transport Industry*, Eyefortransport – First Conference Ltd., www.eyefortransport.com

Hammant, J. (1995), 'Information technology trends in logistics', *Logistics Information Management*, Vol. 8 no. 6, pp. 32-37.

Heaver, T., Meersman, H., Moglia, F., Van de Voorde, E. (2000), 'Do merger and alliances influence European shipping and port competition?', *Maritime Policy & Management*, Vol. 27 no. 4.

Introna, L.D. (1993), 'The impact of information technology on logistics', *Logistics Information Management*, Vol. 6 no. 2, pp. 37-42.

Kia, M., Shayan, E, Ghotb, F. (2000), 'The importance of information technology in port terminal operations', *International Journal of Physical Distribution & Logistics Management*, Vol. 30 no. 3/4, pp. 331-344.

Lee, H.L., Billington, C. (1992), 'Managing supply chain inventory: pitfalls and opportunities', *Sloan Management Review*, Vol. 33 no. 3, pp. 65-73.

Logistics Management & Distribution Report (2000), *Study looks at how carriers use the web*, April, http://www.manufacturing.net

McDonnell, R., Sweeney, E. (2001), 'The role of information technology in the supply chain', *Logistics Solutions*, Issue 4, pp. 9-13.

Merlino, M., Testa, S. (1998), 'L'adozione delle tecnologie dell'informazione nelle aziende fornitrici di servizi logistici dell'area genovese-savonese: risultati di un'indagine empirica', proceedings of the 2nd Workshop *I processi innovativi nella piccola impresa*, 21- 22 May, Urbino, Italy.

Minguzzi, A., Morvillo, A. (1999), 'Entreprenurial culture and the spread of information technology in transport firms. First results on a Southern Italy sample', proceedings of 44th ICSB World Conference *Innovation and Economic Development: the Role of Entrepreneurship and Small and Medium Enterprises*, 20-23 June, Naples, Italy.

OECD (1998), *Measuring the ICT sector*, http://www1.oecd.org/dsti/sti/it/infosoc/index.htm

OECD (1999), *The Economic and Social Impacts of Electronic Commerce: Preliminary Findings and Research Agenda*, http://www1.oecd.org/dsti/sti/it/infosoc/index.htm

Peel, R. (1995), 'Information technology in the express transport industry', *Logistics Information Management*, Vol. 8 no. 3, 18-21.

Politecnico di Milano, Assologistica (2001), *Indagine sull'evoluzione strutturale delle imprese della logistica in Italia*, Department of Economics and Production, May, Milano, Italy.

Pontrandolfo, P., Scozzi, B. (1999), 'Information and Communication Technology and Supply Chain Management: a reasoned taxonomy', proceedings of the *4th International Symposium on Logistics 'Logistics in the information age'*, 11-14 July, Florence, Italy.

Regan, A.C., Song, J. (2001), 'An industry in transition: third party logistics in the information age', paper given at the *Transportation Research Board, 80th Annual Meeting*, January, Washington DC, USA.

Rockwell, B. (1999), 'Seamless Global Logistics and the Internet', presentation given at *Electronic Commerce for Freight Transportation Conference*, 3rd June, New Orleans, USA.

SMAU Ricerche (2001), *Osservatorio SMAU sull'ICT 2001*, Franco Angeli, Milano, Italy.

Stough, R.R. (2001), 'New technologies in logistics management', in Brewer *et al.* (ed.) *Handbook of Logistics and Supply Chain Management*, Elsevier Science Ltd, p. 517.

Tilanus, B. (1997), *Information Systems in Logistics and Transportation*, IFORS Conference, Göteburg, Sweden.

TRILOG (1999), *Europe End Report*, The TRILOG-Europe Consortium, October, Delft, The Netherlands.

UNCTAD (2000), *Review of Maritime Transport*, United Nations, p. 84.

Chapter 3

Education and Training Provision in the Field of Logistics and Transport in Italy

Immacolata Vellecco

Introduction

The dynamics of providing training in the field of logistics and transport reflects the general trend which, over recent years, has marked the Italian education and training system.

In Italy, a considerable gap has emerged between, on the one hand, the range of integrated skills required in all professional roles and, on the other, the theoretical knowledge provided by secondary school and University. High levels of youth unemployment already manifest in the 1980s highlighted the growing inadequacy of the school and University to meet the real needs of industry.

This has led to an ever-increasing need for additional training programmes beyond the secondary school cycle, aimed at completing the specialised training of young people and with a view to bringing together occupational supply and demand.

A substantial supply of post-secondary school training has consequently been developed in an attempt to establish a much closer link between the school and the world of employment.

Likewise, since the end of the 1980s, University education has also undergone a process of innovation over and above traditional degree courses. This has included the introduction of University diploma courses and the growth of numerous Master's courses.

Italian Universities have now entered a final process of reform and alignment to European standards which, once in place, should lead to an improvement of final profile standards. This, in turn, should ensure greater occupational access through the enhancement of career guidance and closer links with industry.

The phase of rapid expansion within the system has been boosted by the availability of financial resources and by the improved utilisation of European funding on the part of Regional Authorities.

These dynamics have led to an increase in training programmes, very diverse in content, duration and typology of user, as well as in didactic objectives (Figure 3.1). This has also generated fierce competition between the different institutions (academic/non-academic) that operate within the training sector, owing to the ease with which new training providers have become involved. Whilst representing the interests of their members (trade associations, Chambers of Commerce etc.), some institutions traditionally active in the business training sector have also diversified their activity towards youth training.

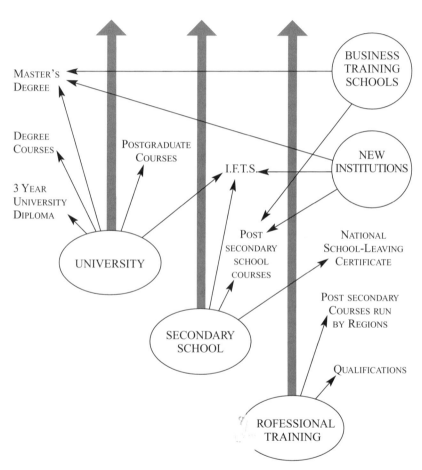

Figure 3.1 The education and training system in Italy

The lack of co-ordination of the above initiatives has, moreover, necessitated a complete reorganisation of the system, so as to ensure functional effectiveness in the employment market and conformity to European standards.

Insofar as international competition of production is concerned, the above dynamics have had greater impact upon those more critical disciplinary areas which have encountered a much more urgent demand for human resources able to satisfy the fast-changing working context.

The supply of training in business logistics and transport, for example, fully reflects the general trend which may be applied to the entire training system in Italy, in that logistics and transportation are among the most crucial activities for companies and the entire national economic system to be competitive. For such activities, there has been clear and pressing evidence of the lack of human resources able to promote and sustain innovative processes.

After a brief description of the training needs linked to logistics integration (see Section 'Training needs and business areas'), this paper analyses the supply of training for the logistics and transport industry.

Following a description of the national secondary school certificates and traditional degree courses provided by the education system, attention is then focused on additional courses that have expanded and modernised the supply (Section 'The education division: courses and professional profiles'). The activities of training bodies (see Section 'The training division: institutions, typologies of courses and course subjects') involved in both business and youth training is then examined.

Finally, the new framework called *Formazione Integrata Superiore (F.I.S.)* is illustrated (see Section 'Integrated advanced technical training'). Objectives and contents of courses set in place in the first two years of activating the new system are described.

The overall picture obtained is that of a system in transformation, whose reorganisation processes are governed by flexibility and alliance mechanisms.

Training Needs and Business Areas

In the field of logistics and transportation, the determinants of training needs are connected to new professional figures who will be able to integrate the activities and processes both within the company itself and between companies; in other words, the ability to operate transversally and to enhance the company's potential through its information and production tools and technologies.

The new needs derive principally from the transformation of the relationship with suppliers, in which greater relevance is attributed to the information and operational services and their role in the development and delivery of the product (De Toni, Nassimbeni, 1994). In particular, this determines:

♦ the need for production planning and control systems to be redefined and made compatible;
♦ the need for more sophisticated tools of co-ordination and control for the selection of suppliers and evaluation of their performance, so as to maintain a high tension towards improvement.

It is, of course, rare for responsibility relating to the different areas of logistics to be concentrated in one individual. In manufacturing firms that have complex production processes or that make use of outsourcing services, there is usually a materials manager present, while firms which produce and distribute convenience goods tend to use a distribution manager, similar to commercial firms and those providing services (Urgeletti Tinarelli, 1998).

In large production and commercial organisations, the figure of the buyer is frequently found; this requires high profile human resources who also possess operational capabilities. The buyer is required to possess knowledge of the markets and the ability to negotiate sub-suppliers by checking the technical and production modalities, as well as contractual agreements in a global market. Moreover, the close relationship between the buyer and production on the one hand, and marketing on the other, require that he/she possess the ability to establish good relations.

Small firms have to reorganise the main business activities (production, marketing and logistics), in order to increase efficiency levels and integration of logistics with modern distribution. The crucial elements, therefore, are guaranteed high quality standards of production (to be monitored and sustained over time) and the ability to provide an appropriate commercial service.

In short, as complexity is increased, new skills and resources are required by small and medium-sized enterprises (SMEs) to operate on the market.

The growing availability of information management support systems and the new combinations of skills and functionality make the choice of support software even more complex, while it seems no longer possible to postpone the training of professionals needed to manage these new tools (Ayers, 1999).

The trend towards a unified view of logistics in manufacturing and commercial systems is significantly reflected in the organisation and management of transport companies. They are, in fact, called upon to manage the synchronisation of physical flow at different stages of the logistics-production cycles, through integrated services in the transfer of goods from one point in the territory to another (Vito, 1995). The outsourcing of transportation, however, does not preclude the need for continued updating of personnel, capable of negotiating and managing transport contracts in the light of new rules and regulations regarding single means of transport (Augello, 1998).

On the other hand, for transport operators, the need to acquire better management skills becomes all the more evident, the purpose being to expand, segment and differentiate their services, while appropriately weighing up costs and income. Equally important is the development of good relationship skills and their role in setting up long term alliances intended to progressively substitute occasional transactions (Marien, 1996).

With regard to industrial districts, 'a policy of state-private training is becoming more and more necessary, the aim being to develop interface professional figures who would operate both in private firms and public agencies. They would also be capable of managing business problems and public space, and have a complete overview of the training supply' (Bologna, 1997).

Basically, 'it is difficult to define with precision the professional profile of a logistics manager. Historically, this activity has attracted specialists in mathematics and statistics, people from a background of informatics with an operational application, and people working in commercial distribution. The numbers concerned are certainly insufficient in relation to the demand which the market generates and will continue to generate over the coming years' (Merlino, 2000).

Top logistics managers should, in any case, possess a wider[1] range of skills than in the past. In the area of specialised logistics skills, results of research (Murphy, Poist, 1998) have shown the importance of non-traditional skills – Customer Service, Distribution Communication, Demand Forecasting, Production Planning, International Logistics[2] – alongside traditional[3] skills, thus confirming logistics management as an inter-functional activity, intended to interact with subjects internal and external to the firm, and in close connection with marketing functions.

With reference to raising the level of logistics awareness within the national economic system, three closely-related objectives appear to be significant:

♦ to guarantee young people joining firms as management trainees or support staff a higher level of logistics culture than in the past;
♦ to update the knowledge of senior and middle managers, as well as operational staff;
♦ to provide training for researchers and consultants, who would ensure the aggregation and dissemination of know-how, namely the development and implementation of new methodologies and tools for business management.

The first objective is also typical of Master's programmes and youth training courses financed by the European Social Fund (ESF).

The second objective is carried out in the traditional *business* sector, i.e. through business training courses, generally of a short period (a few days to a maximum of a few weeks). These courses are of two types:

♦ 'custom', consisting in training courses designed and delivered to meet the needs, problems and business culture of the client;
♦ 'catalogue', organised by training institutions according to the size of the company, the level of responsibility and/or the functional area of the participant.

The third objective seems to be linked to the nurturing of a virtuous cycle between research, consultancy and training. This is achieved through the contribution of workshops, seminars and conferences organised in collaboration with industry.

How these objectives are reached through a structured range of training options will be described in the following paragraphs.

The Education Division: Courses and Professional Profiles

Technical-professional Secondary Education

Italian students enter secondary school at the age of fourteen, after two cycles of education: *junior school* (five years, from the age of six) and middle school (three years, from the age of eleven).

Secondary school has many lines of studies (classic, scientific, technical, administrative, and so on) and is ruled by the Ministry of Education. Studies duration is usually of five years at the end of which students get a secondary-school diploma.

As far as concerns logistics and transport, the secondary school that has traditionally prepared pupils for employment in the maritime transport sector is the *Istituto Tecnico Nautico*. Two qualifications can be attained:

♦ Maritime transport technician;
♦ Maritime equipment and plant technician.

The training of the *Maritime transport technician* centres on the acquisition of knowledge and working methods for organising transport, through studies allowing the professional to also enter the inter-modal transport sector.[4]

Individuals trained according to the second profile, *Maritime equipment and plant technician*, can be placed in the sectors concerned with the management of thermic, electrical, mechanical and fluid-dynamic plants, with particular reference to naval propulsion and plant engineering.[5]

The length of courses at the *Istituto Tecnico Nautico* (about thirty institutes in Italy) is five years. It is also possible to gain qualifications linked to transport and maritime activity (maritime specialist, naval mechanic) after three years of study at *Istituti Professionali per l'Industria e l'Artigianato* (specialised secondary schools for industry and trades).

While the courses offered by the *Istituto Tecnico Nautico* have always been of a highly specific nature, the same cannot be said for the whole secondary education system.

In the face of the changing demand for professionalism by industry, the aim of the education system has been to expand and strengthen basic education so as to develop transversal and multivalent professional skills, rather than specific professional skills. Professional specialisation has, therefore, been placed in a training phase beyond secondary education.

In order to reconstruct a closer link between secondary education and the business environment, post-secondary courses were initiated towards the mid-1980s to try, through both content and business training experience, to bring school leavers closer to the production sector which would be prepared to employ them. Training has been directed towards young people in possession of a national secondary school certificate in the technical, industrial or commercial field, or with a traditional secondary school certificate.[6]

Training interventions aiming at the acquisition of technical competencies of sectoral nature were run by secondary schools (in the form of post-secondary courses) or, to a larger extent, by professional training centres (Regional vocational training courses).

These training typologies constitute the area in which the integration between training bodies and firms has begun experimentation. Post-secondary and Regional courses are generally based on collaboration with the business world, and are centred mainly on defining ways of setting up work placements.

In the transport sector, one of the earliest experiments was 'Nautisud', a post-secondary course for technical-maritime trainees started in 1995. The aim was for the student to acquire specific professional competence on the ship itself and of related tasks, through familiarisation with the ship and the organisation of work on board.[7]

Other post-secondary courses have targeted the growing importance of logistics and related technological support in both business[8] and transport management, from a specific transport mode perspective,[9] and from the point of view of logistics integration.[10]

Experimental projects aimed at revising course programmes and didactics in the *Istituti Tecnici Professionali* (technical professional schools) have begun since early '90s in many schools, financed by European Union funds.

Higher level post-secondary and non-university training is currently planned by the Regions within the new FIS framework, whose objective is to ensure greater coordination within the system, to improve efficiency, in terms of its usefulness to the employment market, and to conform to European standards (see Section 'Integrated advanced technical training').

University Education

Up until the end of the 1980s, Italian Universities awarded only one type of qualification (degree) at the end of a four or five-year study programme.

The main University preparing professionals specifically for the transport sector, particularly maritime transport, has traditionally been the *Istituto Universitario Navale, Naples*.[11] Whilst being the principal pole of attraction for university courses in Economics in Campania Region, this University still preserves the specialised features of its degree courses.

At the faculty of Nautical Sciences the degree course in *Nautical Sciences* provides specialised options in Oceanography, Geodesy, Navigation and Radio Electronics. More recently (academic year 1993/94), the degree course in *Environmental Sciences* (with special options in Marine Studies and the Atmosphere) has been launched.

The degree course in *Maritime and Transport Economics* is today one of the four courses in the Faculty of Economics; the latter has progressively expanded and diversified[12] its own training objectives.

The graduate in *Maritime and Transport Economics* goes on to employment in firms dealing in maritime transport and services related to transport (insurance, maritime agencies, freight-carrying firms), but may also cover the role of business accountant or take part in any of the state-run competitions open to graduates of other economics courses.

A further course in *Maritime and Transport Economics* has been run by the Faculty of Economics at the University of Genoa since the 1994/5 academic year.

With this new degree course, the University of Genoa has made an important contribution to sustain the development of the port of Genoa. The course has been set up to satisfy the needs of maritime operators, asking for technical, managerial and cultural training.

The increase in plant engineering technology demanded by competition, the geographical growth of markets and the ever more complex problems related to human resource management have nonetheless pointed to an emerging gap in the University system to meet the needs of industry.

Attempts to achieve higher occupational objectives for professional profiles have been made, on the one hand, through the establishment of new degree courses, while there have also been newly designed training initiatives, such as University diplomas and Master's programmes.[13]

University diplomas have tried to bridge the gap in the first phase of alignment of the Italian university system to that of other European Union countries.

University diplomas have been based on the collaboration between universities, firms and the local context and on a didactic model alternating between university-based study and experience in the field, in a three-year study cycle.

The purpose was to prepare qualified technicians who would combine practical and theoretical knowledge, would be able to rapidly gain employment in production, and would have the tools to keep pace with technological innovation in their individual sector. It should, however, be noted that the University diploma courses did not give automatic access to degree courses.

Furthermore, in response to the need for preparation in the area of *Engineering Management* which was becoming more and more apparent by the mid-1970s, the University diploma in *Operations and Logistics Management*[14] was established. Subsequently, the degree course in *Engineering Management*[15] was launched, to achieve the objective of incorporating managerial competencies at the core of an inter-sectoral engineering preparation, which would facilitate the dissemination of technological innovation within firms.

The picture described above, however, appears to have entered a final stage as a result of the implementation of the University Reform.[16] Two successive study cycles – the first of three years, the second of two – are encompassed in the new regulations, allowing each university ample autonomy in outlining professional profiles and in structuring the teaching. Courses evolving from the application of the Reform and from competition between universities urged by the Reform will adhere even more closely to the training requirements of industry.

The Training Division: Institutions, Typologies of Courses and Course subjects

This division traditionally identifies the business area of managerial training and incorporates courses of both the 'custom' and 'catalogue' type. Moreover, the dynamics of the training system (see 'Introduction') have led to a breakdown of barriers between this business area and youth training, thereby ensuring that many institutions develop an almost complete range of courses.

In this division 15 training bodies of varying type have been identified as active in the field of logistics and transport. In the first group are to be found one University and three academic spin-off Institutions which were set up specifically to focus on business training. Merging academic teaching experience with a continuous updating of knowledge through research has meant that these Institutions are able to take part in the training of researchers and consultants new to the field. The widely recognised standard of the courses also creates a reference point for local and national business associations.

Belonging to this group are:

♦ University Consortium MIP, the Polytechnic of Milan;
♦ *Centro Universitario di Organizzazione Aziendale* (CUOA Foundation), to which belong universities, public and private bodies and trade associations of Vicenza;
♦ *Scuola di Direzione Aziendale* (SDA) of the Bocconi University of Milan;

♦ *Libera Università degli Studi 'Carlo Cattaneo' di Castellana* (LIUC).

Because of their direct links with universities, the following should be included in this group:

♦ *Istituto per lo Studio dei Trasporti nell'Integrazione Economica Europea* (I.S.T.I.E.E.) Trieste, predominantly concerned with research;
♦ *Istituto di Studi Direzionali* (ISTUD), management school in Milan, founded by firms and trade associations;
♦ SOGEA, a syndicate set up jointly by the trade federations of Liguria, trade associations and the University of Genoa.

Another group consists of those institutions promoted by the Chambers of Commerce, Industry, Agriculture and Artisanal products. To this group belong:

♦ *Istituto di Formazione Operatori Aziendali* (IFOA), Training and Services Department of the Chambers of Commerce;
♦ *Scuola Nazionale dei Trasporti* (SNT), La Spezia.

A final group is made up of different bodies and associations, including:

♦ *Associazione Italiana di Logistica e Supply Chain Management* (AILOG) a professional association including purchasing managers, entrepreneurs and academics;
♦ *Associazione Italiana di Management degli Approvvigionamenti* (ADACI), a professional association including purchasing managers;
♦ *Istituto Superiore di Formazione e Ricerca per i Trasporti* (ISFORT), a public limited company set up by Italian National Railways;
♦ *Centro Studi, Ricerche e Formazione sui Trasporti, Ambiente e Mobilità* (CERTAM), a trade union association;
♦ Syndicate for the training and development of SMEs (COFIMP), a training body of the Association for Small Enterprises, Bologna;
♦ *Istituto di Ricerca Internazionale* (IIR), the Italian branch of the IIR Group – Institute for International Research – the largest world organisation for business information, a leading private multinational company.[17]

The strength of the Institutions belonging to the latter two groups lies in the fact that, while they are an expression of the business environment, they enjoy close links with operators' training needs.

It should be noted that all the Institutions are located in northern Italy, except for ISFORT and CERTAM based in Rome. Even though this territorial distribution is a consequence of the gap existing in the country in terms of training demand, it also shows the disproportion of training provision for operators.

As Figure 3.2 shows, SDA Bocconi, ADACI, ISFORT, IIR and AILOG provide a restricted range of business training (custom and catalogue) in the form of short courses, whereas ISTUD, IFOA, SOGEA and the National School of Transport, boast a nearly complete range.

TRAINING BODIES	LOCATION	MASTER'S COURSES	EUROPEAN SOCIAL FUND YOUTH TRAINING COURSES	BUSINESS TRAINING		SEMINARS AND WORKSHOPS
				CATALOGUE	CUSTOM	
ADACI	Milano			■		■
AILOG	Milano			■		■
CERTAM	Roma		■		■	■
COFIMP	Bologna	■		■		■
CUOA	Vicenza	■		■		
IIR	Milano			■		■
IFOA	Reggio Emilia			■		■
ISFORT	Roma			■		■
I.S.T.I.E.E.	Trieste					■
ISTUD	Milano	■		■		■
LIUC	Varese	■				■
MIP	Milano	■		■		■
S. N. Trasporti	La Spezia	■		■		■
SDA Bocconi	Milano			■		■
SOGEA	Genova	■		■		■

Figure 3.2 Training bodies/courses in business and youth training

In the portfolio of courses offered by MIP, CUOA, CERTAM and COFIMP, there can be found combinations of short and long courses.

Seminars and workshops oriented towards the exchange of knowledge and experience between managers and researchers/consultants are to be found in the portfolio of many institutions, particularly those involved in research.

Several bodies (MIP, CUOA, SDA, ADACI, AILOG) have concentrated their activity on courses for firms in the industrial and business sectors; in prime position are the courses devoted to production technology – a central element leading to organisational innovation – and to the integration of processes within the firm and between firms. The National School of Transport, ISFORT, CERTAM and ISTIEE, on the other hand, concentrate on transportation issues.

Master's Programmes and other Youth Training Courses

The Institutions offering Master's programmes are MIP, CUOA, ISTUD, SOGEA, IFOA, LIUC, COFIMP and the National School of Transport.[18] The Master in *Business Engineering Management* at MIP works from the assumption that the preparation of the traditional engineer should incorporate management training. The programme includes the study of business administration oriented towards managing and running an organisation, with particular attention focused on technological innovation.

In the Master's programme in *Integrated Business Management* at CUOA, specialized study of Logistics and Production is available as an option[19] for students on the course.

At CUOA, there are also Youth Training courses financed by ESF. The course for *Logistics Manager* is designed to train professional figures capable of running the integrated management of materials flow, problems related to the production and distribution of the finished product, including those deriving from de-localised production, and purchasing and supply both within and outside the EU.

In the area of courses related to commercial distribution there is the Master's in *Distribution Management* at IFOA, a post-graduate specialised course focusing on management areas of distribution firms, and on trade marketing for industrial firms. Also on offer at IFOA is the Master's course in *Logistics and Production Integration*, and a post-secondary course for *Technicians in automated production*.

At ISTUD, the three editions of the Master's in *Logistics and Global Economics* have had considerable success. The course is intended for students who have graduated or are about to graduate. The specific modules cover subjects related to transport management and logistic systems re-design.

Courses at SOGEA have attempted to go beyond the purely sectoral formulation of the transport concept (ship, railway, air, road haulage) by adopting a *systemic* view, where efficient and effective client service is the result of linking together different stages of transportation.

Among post-graduate courses on offer are the Master's in *Port Studies and Logistics* (1997/98), and in Logistics (1996/97 and 1995/96), which have been recently substituted by Master's courses focusing on the business application of information technology (1998/99), while among post-secondary courses there is the *Euro-shipping project*[20] to train technicians in the maritime sector (1997/98).

The *Scuola Nazionale Trasporti e Logistica* in La Spezia has strengthened its position in certain areas and priority subjects, such as logistics, transport and inter-modality, the environment, innovative technologies, customs and legislation, human resources and business economics. The School has also set up Master's programmes focused on information systems applied to logistics, quality management in transport companies and environmental issues. For the training of secondary school-leavers (aged 18), the most significant initiatives have been the courses for *Administrators in Maritime and inter-modal transport and in Business management for transport companies*.

The youth training programmes at CERTAM have been run under European Projects and have focused on new technologies in the air transport sector and on safety.

In recent years there have been new initiatives focusing on the need to train managers on Information Technology applications, both at the strategic and operational level. As well as the recent Master's programmes at SOGEA already mentioned, in this area should also be included the Master's in *E-business and Supply Chain Management* at LIUC and the Master's in *Supply Net Management* at COFIMP. The Master's in *E-business and Supply Chain Management* at LIUC[21] has been designed in close collaboration with companies and aims to provide students with the following:

♦ elements enabling them to contribute to the definition of business strategies, with particular regard to the opportunities made available by ICT in the area of the Supply Chain;
♦ a fund of specialised technical competencies with regard to the practical application of ICT in the Supply Chain, for example, managing the introduction of a Supply Chain Planning (SCP) data processing system in a manufacturing firm.

The Master's in *Supply Net Management* at COFIMP provides Supply Net training for professionals who need to be able to design and manage a business logistics system and to structure the business supply net by harmonising the functions of Enterprise Resource Planning (ERP) business applications.

In-company Training: Custom and Catalogue Courses

In the area of business training it was found that almost all the training bodies offered courses. Some of them, the great management schools (CUOA, SDA) or various bodies strongly geared towards training (IFOA, IIR, COFIMP) have introduced the subjects of business logistics to complete and bring up to date the range of catalogue courses on offer. For some of these, (SDA, IFOA, IIR) custom training is also important.

In other bodies, training runs alongside research activity and consultancy, thus developing significant synergy with the latter two. In some cases training represents a particularly well-established business, thus allowing for *catalogue* courses to be run (ISTUD, ISFORT, ADACI, COFIMP); in other cases less structured courses are run, such as seminars and workshops (I.S.T.I.E.E.) or they are more strictly subject to the request of specific companies (CERTAM).

The *Scuola di Direzione Aziendale* at the Bocconi University in Milan holds a prominent position. The courses dedicated to operations managers have been developed within the Technology Area.

Moreover a series of seminars and courses to order have been identified dealing with different aspects of the subject of logistics-production integration.

Other courses relating to integrated logistics management are run within the Information Systems Area. One special initiative named 'ERP School' has been launched in collaboration with KPMG Consulting in response to the current needs of professionals and consultants in the field of implementation of the main Enterprise Resource Planning packages.

Courses worthy of note are also to be found at MIP which monitors the most up-to-date technical innovations in manufacturing and logistics at the international level. The evening course 'Technological choices and business management' responds to the needs of graduates in engineering or in other scientific and economics disciplines who would like to develop their managerial training parallel to their working activity.

MIP also runs training initiatives, designed and delivered to meet the specific needs of the clients. Consultancy activity takes into account the results of applied research conducted by MIP and enables direct assessment of the validity of innovations.

The CUOA Foundation[22] organises courses for functional areas of business through *CUOA Impresa*, the Division whose role is to provide firms with high quality training, research and consultancy. The Division is also specialised in the area of Production, Logistics and Quality and offers refresher modules including:

♦ international transportation of goods: regulations, responsibility and criteria for selecting carriers;
♦ purchasing and techniques for supplier evaluation;
♦ order cycle management.

In the *catalogue* training programmes organised at ISTUD, subjects related to logistics integration are dealt with as part of the modules dedicated to operational processes and include:

♦ purchasing management;
♦ physical distribution and outsourcing;
♦ re-thinking the supply chain;
♦ cost reduction and improvement of time to market.

The training proposals at IFOA respond to the need for small and medium-sized firms to set up logistics design and management and integrate them with manufacturing. The specific objective is to improve the flow of materials, from the supplier to the delivery of the finished product to the customer, through the control and acceleration of the production stages, thereby reducing surplus stocks and diseconomies. Such objectives are reached either by training initiatives, or by consultancy and other business services.[23]

AILOG offers strategic and specialised courses lasting two days, focussing on supply chain management, logistics auditing and e-logistics. It also provides consultancy services and promotes conferences, meetings and work-groups on logistics issues. A special section of AILOG is devoted to foster logistics culture among students and junior partners.

The IIR conducts Professional Training through its Training Division. The participants acquire the techniques and tools to manage time and methods related to the production of goods or the delivery of services that make best use of human resources and tools. The content also takes into consideration any future legal implications tied to the application of the laws in force. With regard to conferences,[24] the most frequently and repeatedly studied subjects are: supply chain re-engineering, evaluation and management of suppliers, application of ERP systems, optimisation of customer relations and the negotiation of transport contracts.

Training activity at ADACI, run since 1999 by ADACI Formanagement S.r.l., is aimed at those employed in the Supplies and Materials management sector. The courses are at different levels of specialisation and offer opportunities both for those who are beginning a career in this field, and for those with experience who have already reached a certain level of responsibility. For Members, training covers the units necessary to obtain Certification for the professions of *Purchaser* and *Materials*

Manager, according to the procedure set down by the relevant Association.

ADACI Formanagement also designs and carries out specific consultancy and in-house training interventions, aimed at satisfying precise business needs.

The catalogue courses at COFIMP are organised into flexible modules, each of 8 or 5 hours. In the Technical Area, there are courses for business managers and people with responsibility, based on the principal subjects of business logistics. In addition, COFIMP organises courses for specific business needs and consultancy services.

Seminar cycles for senior and middle managers are organised by the *Scuola Nazionale dei Trasporti* at the request of firms, on subjects such as quality management and certification in transport companies, warehousing organisation and management, regulations and customs problems relating to exchanges with EU and non-EU countries.

The need for training and development of managerial know-how in the transport sector is dealt with by ISFORT, whose purpose is to produce and to promote a high level of knowledge in the transport sector and, more generally, in the movement of people, goods and information. The training consists in flexible and differentiated initiatives – from one-day workshops to seminars lasting two or more weeks – in response to the requirements of the clients, who are those firms offering or requesting transport services. The subjects range from the evaluation and analysis of projects, cost analysis, outsourcing strategies, quality service management and customer satisfaction, to safety at work, the formulation and realisation of mobility strategies, the management and maintenance of transport and infrastructure.

I.S.T.E.E. is involved in the study and promotion of transport research within the European Union, as well as relations between the Union and Developing countries. One essential element of the Institute's activity in the European Union is the organisation of annual international seminars involving academics and specialists from various countries.

Training courses at CERTAM aim to promote projects in the transport, environment and mobility sectors. The aim is the understanding of trends linked to the development of European and international policies. Meetings, seminars, conferences and study days are organised; training and refresher courses for all employees in the sector are also designed and managed. Research and consultancy services are conducted in collaboration with public bodies, research institutes and managers of transport companies.

Integrated Advanced Technical Training

For several years, post-secondary school, non-university training has been planned and overseen by the Regions within a new framework called *Formazione Superiore Integrata* (FIS).

The Regions conduct analyses of the demand for advanced and intermediate level professionalism and consequently outline frameworks for new training initiatives.

Integrated advanced technical training courses (IFTS) are the main innovation of FIS. In fact, FIS is concerned with a new branch of post-secondary training which is not a continuation of secondary school education, nor is it related to training courses of the Region or to university courses.

The courses[25] are co-financed by the Ministry of Education (L.440/97) and the Region through the European Social Fund.

For access to the courses, open to both employed and unemployed young people and adults, a secondary school leaving certificate is usually required. Alternatively, in some cases the possession of specific competencies acquired directly in the workplace is considered valid.

The courses are designed and run by a pool of actors, among whom the following have to take part:

♦ a secondary school;
♦ a professional training agency or centre;
♦ a University;
♦ one or more firms, or a consortium or association of firms.

Institutions are encouraged to become involved, not on a competitive basis, but rather according to a network aimed at enhancing both the individual strengths and synergy which the actors together are capable of creating. Collaboration between actors in the pool, in fact, restores to each of them a role consonant with their specific competencies.

The didactic approach should provide the right balance between lessons based on theory and those based on practice. It also includes work placement constituting at least 30% of the total number of hours in firms. At least 50% of the teaching body must come from industry and the professions.

Each course must be structured into defined and autonomous modules. Credits for modules attended are recorded in a training booklet and are recognised in the case of further university study, or may be used directly in the world of employment.

Of the 221 initiatives financed in 1998, 22 (i.e. 10%) dealt with transport and logistics, further 17 initiatives were concerned with the dissemination of new information and communication technologies, the management of information systems and networks within and between firms; 3 initiatives focused on the business integration of organisational processes, 16 on production, automation and control processes, 12 on the control, certification and management of quality business systems, 5 on the management of the agro-industrial *filière*.[26]

Within the courses focusing on transport, there is a remarkable variety of professional profiles: terminal manager, port-related business technician, specialist in logistics and inter-modal transport, technician specialised in telecommunications systems and networks applied to the transportation of goods.

As far as concerns final professional profiles and typologies of business to which the former are directed, it may be seen (Figure 3.3) that greater attention has been focused on training individuals to run transport systems or port, airport and inland hubs, as well as on training technicians to work in port-related firms. Fewer courses have been devoted specifically to the maritime mode or to objectives of a general nature connected to logistics integration and inter-modality. Eight out of twenty-two courses were conducted in southern Italy.

In 1999 there were 17 courses out of a total of 395 on transportation, corresponding to approximately 4%.[27]

PROVIDERS

- SPECIALIST SECONDARY SCHOOLS
- UNIVERSITIES
- PROFESSIONAL TRAINING CENTRES AND AGENCIES
- BUSINESS CONSORTIUM

GEOGRAPHICAL AREA

NORTH	11
CENTRE	3
SOUTH	8

PROFILES FOR THE TRANSPORT SECTORS (1998)

- TECHNICIAN TRAINED TO RUN AND INTEGRATE THE TRANSPORT SYSTEM (5 COURSES)
- TECHNICIAN TRAINED TO RUN TRANSPORT HUBS (8 COURSES)
- TECHNICIAN FOR PORT-RELATED FIRMS (4 COURSES)
- SPECIALIST TECHNICIAN IN LOGISTICS INTEGRATION AND INTERMODALITY (3 COURSES)
- TECHNICIAN FOR ON-BOARD/DECK EQUIPMENT AND NAVIGATION ASSISTANCE (1 COURSE)
- MERCHANT NAVY OFFICER (1 COURSE)

Figure 3.3 Integrated training courses (I.F.T.S.)

Conclusions

The analysis carried out highlights the inflexibility of the education system in relation to the evolving professionalism required by the industrial world.

Current initiatives in secondary education have not reformed training, but rather have put off training in specific professional skills to a later stage.

Italian Universities have produced some noteworthy innovations, especially where close links have been forged with the industrial world. At the present moment, a process of change is underway as a result of the reform; this process brings into question the innovations already achieved (in particular, the degree courses in *Engineering management* and the diploma courses in *Operations and Logistics Management*) but, at the same time, constitutes a great opportunity to renew the Faculties and degree courses, and to redefine professional profiles in the light of the new requirements of the industrial world.

The training system has, on the other hand, brought about numerous initiatives.

The training courses and initiatives described in Sections 'The training division: institutions typologies of courses and course subjects' and 'Integrated advanced technical training' highlight a remarkable variety of content which may be attributed to several large-scale topics, namely:

♦ the integration of production with other business functions, and with supply and distribution functions;

♦ integration between firms and purchasing and supply management;
♦ the management of the transport stage with a view to integrating the supply chain.

Industrial firms, under pressure to gain competitive margins in the international context, have contributed to the development of initiatives focused on production technologies and on the integration of processes within and between businesses. The great management schools, however, given their ability to set up courses whose content can be shaped to the real and future needs of firms, could, in effect, harness the demand and thereby make such courses a profitable business.

There has even been a considerable number and variety of initiatives focusing on transport, made possible by:

♦ a maturation process in training provision, linked to the development of research on transport and the accumulation of competencies;
♦ greater availability of public training funds, crucial for a sector in which the small size of firms and the cultural characteristics of entrepreneurship would make difficult the activation of privately financed training initiatives;
♦ a policy sought after and actively supported by the collaboration of operators, to contribute to the modernisation and re-launch of the transportation industry.

Insofar as content is concerned, such initiatives tend to conform to an integrated view of the transport system and activity, and in doing so highlight new problems, ranging from the use of advanced support tools to the running of the system and activity of the firms.

One element which emerges strongly is the territorial imbalance of these initiatives, favouring northern over southern Italy. This imbalance, which may also be attributed to the cultural characteristics and size of the local business community, does not appear to be compensated by initiatives such as IFTS courses.

On the basis of this detailed account, it is also possible to identify those elements that are destined to mark the future of the training market and to condition in a decisive way the success and launch of new initiatives. Such elements consist in the active involvement of operators and the flexibility of courses on offer, taking into account both the modular structure of training and the rapid and frequent adaptation of content.

A fundamental condition for success remains, however, related to the preservation of close links between training activity and that of research and consultancy.

Notes

1 In the area of skills for logistics managers, Poist (1984) differentiates between business skills, logistics skills and management skills. The first refer to the knowledge required directly or indirectly to manage the business (marketing, accounting, finance etc.); the second regard studying the various fields of logistics (transport, warehousing, predictions etc.); the latter concern skills (of planning, organisation and control) and personal qualities (enthusiasm, self assertion) of managers.
2 As listed by the Author, in order of importance.
3 Such as Traffic Management, Inventory Control, Warehousing, Order Processing, Transport Regulation.

4 This profile finds its professional outlet in ports, airports and inter-modal transport, in the management of transport companies and freight carriers, the management of information and telecommunications systems of transport organisations, the protection of the coastline from pollution, and the monitoring of marine and land environment, the enhancement and marketing of marine resources, such as Officer of the Merchant Marine and freelance Technician in maritime transport.

5 Possible professional outlets are in the research, drilling, transport, refining and distribution of petroleum products; the management of energy transformation plants, steam production, refrigeration and air conditioning, depollution of the marine and land environment, waste disposal, as well as the management of automated marine and land plant equipment and plants for the enhancement of marine resources.

6 Post-secondary training courses delivered by schools have experienced a large increase over recent years, thanks to the multi-funded programme (1994-99) set up as part of ESF, under supervision of the Ministry of Education; a specific sub-programme has given rise to a considerable number of courses in the Regions, which come under Obiettivo 1 of FSE. Cf. ISFOL report 1998, p.438.

7 The project for 208 new 'nautical technicians' from 22 state technical-nautical institutes in southern Italy was carried out with the collaboration of Ministries, Firms, Schools, Training Centres.

8 Post-secondary courses in *Technical Logistics and movement of goods*; Post-secondary course for *Business Logistics with technical support Technician*.

9 Course for *Trainee Officers*, Course in *Air Navigation Assistant*.

10 Post-secondary courses in *Management Techniques in Road, Air and Maritime Transport; International Transport Operator; Transport Logistics Technician; Specialist in telecommunications networks, applied to transportation of goods*.

11 The name has recently changed to *Università degli Studi di Napoli 'Parthenope'*.

12 In addition to the degree course in *Maritime and Transport Economics*, the Faculty of Economics at the *Istituto Universitario Navale* also runs degree courses in the Economics of International Commerce and Money Markets, *Economics and Business Studies, Business Economics, Economics of Tourism*. The *Istituto Universitario Navale* has expanded its training provision with the foundation of three new Faculties (Jurisprudence, Telecommunication Engineering, Physical Movement Sciences.

13 Master's programmes will be dealt with in the next section.

14 The University diploma in *Operations and Logistics* was launched in the 1999/2000 academic year at the *Libero Istituto Universitario 'Carlo Cattaneo'* (LIUC), the Polytechnic of Milan (Faculty of Engineering at Lecco), Polytechnic of Turin, the Universities of Calabria, Genova (at Savona), Lecce (at Brindisi), Pisa (Faculty of Engineering), Trieste (at Pordenone), Ancona, Bergamo, Bologna.

15 This degree course was run in the 1999/2000 academic year at the Universities of Bari, Bergamo, Bologna, Brescia, Calabria, 'Carlo Cattaneo', Genova, Modena and Reggio Emilia, Naples *'Federico II'*, Padova (at Vicenza), Palermo, Parma, Roma *'Tor Vergata'*, Udine and the Polytechnics of Milan and Turin.

16 Decree n. 509, 3 November 1999, Law implementing teaching autonomy at Universities, published in the Official Gazette n.2, 4 January 2000.

17 From 35 branches worldwide IIR organises more than 4000 conferences a year in 40 countries.

18 The Master's degrees at MIP and CUOA have been awarded accreditation by ASFOR *(Associazione per la Formazione alla Direzione Aziendale)* and, like the Master's at LIUC, are fee-paying but scholarships are available. Other Masters are co-financed by FSE and are non-fee paying.

19 Other options include Marketing, Administration, Control and Finance.

20 This transnational project was set up to include a module on *Shipping Management* in

Liverpool, with the purpose of encouraging the convergence of professional profiles within the EU through contact between operators and port activity with similar yet different features.

21 The Master's course has been designed in accordance with the University Reform.

22 CUOA also serves as the central hub's main channel for the supply of advanced services to the training system in the Veneto Region, 'continuous training', a communication and exchange network for the purpose of monitoring the training needs and training provision in the Region.

23 For example, research and staff selection, assistance in warehouse stock management, assistance in the introduction of planning methods and product launch.

24 Conference here means a 1, 2 or 3-day event, with numerous speakers; workshops are brief (half or full day) and part of conferences, providing an opportunity for in-depth discussion as well as information or training on highly specific aspects of the general theme of the conference. They are conducted by one or two qualified university teachers or consultants. Seminars, on the other hand, are specific meetings for training senior and junior staff. In recent years, conference organisation has been carried out with the support and collaboration of AILOG.

25 In 1998, on average courses lasted 1200 hours (over two to four semesters), with an average of 20 trainees per course.

26 Source: our elaboration of data from the Ministry of Education, http://www.rete.toscana.it:8899/sett/lavoro/fis/ifts.htm

27 Source: Ministry of Education http://www.istruzione.it/argomenti/ifts/fis99 00.htm

References

Augello, W. J. (1998), 'We still need continuing education in transportation', *Logistics Management Distribution Report*, Vol. 37 no. 6, June, p. 31 (1).

Ayers, A.F. (1999), 'What logistics managers need to know about today's complex information systems', *Transportation & Distribution*, Sept., p. 33.

Bologna, S. (1997), 'Una logistica per i distretti industriali', *Logistica Management*, marzo.

De Toni, A., Nassimbeni, G. (1995), 'Service management negli approvvigionamenti', *Sviluppo e Organizzazione*, no.148, Marzo/Aprile.

ISFOL (1998), *Formazione e occupazione in Italia e in Europa*, Franco Angeli.

Marien, E.J. (1996), 'What transportation professionals need to know', *Transportation & Distribution*, Vo. 37 no.1, Jan., p. 61 (2).

Merlino, M. (2000), 'Logistica tanta, logistici pochi', *Logistica & Management*, novembre.

Murphy, P.R., Poist, R.F.jr (1998), 'Skill requirements of senior-level logisticians. Practitioner perspectives', *International Journal of Physical Distribution & Logistics Management*, Vol. 28 no. 4, pp.284-301. Also published in *International Journal of Physical Distribution & Logistics Management*, Vol. 21 no. 3, pp.3-14.

Poist, R.E. (1984), 'Managing logistics in an era of change', *Defense Transportation Journal*, Vol. 40 no. 5, September-October, pp. 22-30.

Urgeletti Tinarelli, G. (1998), 'Il mestiere del logistico', *Logistica Management*, maggio.

Vito, G. (1995), 'Le implicazioni strategiche dell'integrazione logistica', *Economia e Diritto del Terziario*, no. 2.

Web Sites

ADACI http://www.adaci.it/
CERTAM http://www.uni.net/certam/index.htm
CESTOR http://www.cestor.it/guide.htm
COFIMP http://www.cofimp.it/
CUOA http://www.cuoa.it/index.php
I.S.T.I.E.E. http://www.univ.trieste.it/~istiee/
IFOA http://www.ifoa.it/
IIR http://www.iir-italy.it/
ISFORT http://www.isfort.it
Istituto Universitario Navale http://www.uninav.it/
ISTUD http://www.istud.it
LIUC http://www.liuc.it/
Ministero della Pubblica Istruzione http://www.istruzione.it/argomenti/ifts/ne98049.htm
MIP Politecnico di Milano http://www.mip.polimi.it/mip/it/chi/ma_chi.htm
Scuola Nazionale dei Trasporti di La Spezia http://www.cestor.it/enti/snt.htm
SDA Bocconi http://www.sda.uni-bocconi.it/
SOGEA http://www.sogeanet.it/
Università degli Studi di Genova http://www.economia.unige.it/

Chapter 4

The Structure of Transport and Logistics Industry in Southern Italy

Marcella De Martino

Introduction

In today's highly competitive, global marketplace, the pressure on organisations to find new ways to create and deliver value to customers grows ever stronger. In particular, customer service becomes a key differentiator as the sophistication and demands of the customer continually increase.

Traditionally, most organisations have viewed themselves as entities that exist independently from others and, indeed, need to compete with them in order to survive. Nowadays, the globalization of industry, the time compression in the production and delivery process and consequently the customer service explosion have led logistics and transport operators to reconfigure their organisations by focussing on responsiveness, reliability and relationship. This means that to be competitive in such a dynamic environment, the logistics and transport operator has to give value to the customer through the development of *capabilities and competencies* related to the specific supply chain.

The aim of this chapter is to outline those characteristics of logistics and transport operators in southern Italy which deeply affect the competitiveness of firms in such a dynamic market. To this end, a sample investigation was conducted by means of a questionnaire distributed among logistics and transport operators in Campania. After describing the structural characteristics of the Italian logistics and transport market, the results of the empirical survey were evaluated in the light of the main trends previously mentioned.

The Italian Logistics and Transport Market

In this section we trace some of the features of supply and demand for logistics and transport services in Italy by reviewing the most recent surveys and studies on the subject.

An initial key element of demand analysis consists in the *firm's size*, which affects the degree of outsourcing of logistics and transport services. Size assumes great importance in the case of the Italian industrial and commercial system with its high proportion of small and medium firms (henceforth SMEs). The Italian industrial system, in fact, is strongly characterised by a great number of SMEs: out of 3.5 million of firms, 95% have less than 10 employees; only 2,600 of these (less than 0.1%) are large in size, with more than 250 employees (Confetra, 1999a).

The regional location presents a dichotomy between the North and South: the North-west is dominant per number of firms and employees and average number of employees per firm, while the South falls down in relation to the average number of employees per firm (Table 4.1).

Table 4.1 Regional location of Italian firms

	Number of firms	Number of employees	Employees per firm	Firms out of the total	Employees out of the total
North-West (Piemonte, Val d'Aosta, Lombardia, Liguria)	1,038,608	4,852,685	4.67	29.5%	35.2%
North-East (Trentino A. Adige, Veneto, Friuli V. Giulia, Emilia Romagna)	751,016	3,257,888	4.33	21.3%	23.6%
Centre (Toscana, Umbria, Marche, Lazio)	737,776	3,150,937	4.27	21.0%	22.8%
South (Abruzzo, Molise, Campania, Puglia, Basilicata, Calabria)	681,733	1,777,126	2.61	19.4%	12.9%
Sicily	227,052	536,466	2.36	6.4%	3.9%
Sardinia	85,569	228,107	2.66	2.4%	1.7%
Total	**3,521,754**	**13,803,209**	**3.92**	**100.0%**	**100.0%**

Source: ISTAT, 1997

It is well known that the larger the firm size, the greater the propensity towards outsourcing and logistics innovation.

Indeed, larger industrial and commercial firms are more dynamic in dealing with logistics than small firms. The entrepreneurial culture prevailing in SMEs, however, is characterised by a low sensitivity to the changing external environment, and this naturally affects the degree of outsourcing of logistics and transport services. While large firms tend to retain close control over outsourced activities by means of partnerships with suppliers of services, SMEs are tied to their own service suppliers by shorter and less structured supply relations (CSST, 1997).

Taking into account the importance of size and geographical location of Italian SMEs, it is possible to highlight a number of differences related to the qualitative characteristics of the demand for transport and logistics services. In fact, though a considerable proportion of small firms reflects a fragmented demand for logistics and transport services, for a specific group of SMEs generally operating in an industrial district,[1] such demand is more dynamic. These usually deal with a niche market and require specific transport and logistics services (Federtrasporto, 1997).

Their competitiveness depends on the advantages of co-operation and co-ordination at specific stages of the same supply chain, and on their ability to be cost-effective.

Export-oriented activity is predominant in those SMEs that have a well-developed network of relationships both horizontally (with firms that produce the same product) and vertically (with firms that supply goods or services *downstream* or *upstream* of the supply chain) (MarketLine International, 1997).

The demand for logistics and transport services from such SMEs, therefore, gives rise to a high degree of outsourcing (logistics services other than transport) if the supplier is able to satisfy their requirements in terms of cost and quality of service.

However, the main weakness of the Italian industrial system is the strong heterogeneity of firms; apart from the industrial districts, there is a substantial number of SMEs that (Bologna, 1997):

♦ produce for the local market without an entrepreneurial culture oriented towards internationalisation;
♦ are sub-suppliers of foreign firms and therefore pay little attention to distribution systems.

The inefficiency of such a system (small size, geographical dispersion of firms, and a highly fragmented demand) has been one of the main factors contributing to the slow development of the logistics service business.

Indeed, while it has recorded particularly risk international growth rates, in Italy the outsourcing of such activities has not proceeded apace (Table 4.2).

Table 4.2 The degree of outsourcing of logistics activities in Europe

Country	1997	2002 (Forecast)	Δ%
UK	34%	37%	+9%
France	27%	33%	+22%
BENELUX	25%	28%	+12%
Germany	23%	28%	+22%
Sweden	22%	26%	+18%
Denmark	20%	24%	+20%
Spain	18%	23%	+28%
Italy	13%	16%	+23%

Source: MarketLine International ('EU Logistics', 1997)

Transport is the first activity to be outsourced by Italian industrial and commercial firms, while other logistics activities, like warehousing and inventory, packaging, and quality control, are still managed in house. The transport activity mostly outsourced is downstream of the supply chain; this situation could show an increasing interest of Italian firms in outbound logistics due to its economic impact on the final price of goods (Table 4.3). Inbound logistics, on the other hand, is a crucial activity for large firms that, thanks to their bargaining power, can control the procurement of raw materials and semi-finished goods through stable relationships with suppliers (Censis, 1998).

Table 4.3 Degree of logistics outsourcing in Italy

Degree of outsourcing of some logistics functions:	
Purchasing Transport	74%
Distribution Transport	82%
Freight Transport Clearance	68%
Freight Warehouse and Storage	33%
Product Collection and Loading	23%
Quality Control	7%
Packaging, Labelling, Pricing	13%
Others (EDP, Invoicing, ...)	10%

Source: CSST, 1997

Freight transport clearance has also a high degree of outsourcing because it is traditionally a service supplied by freight forwarders. Freight warehousing and storage are, however, too important to be outsourced; in particular, only large firms have adopted just-in-time production to reduce and rationalise stock and inventory costs. Finally, quality control, product collection and loading, packaging, labelling and pricing are still managed in house by most Italian firms.

Inasmuch as it reflects demand characteristics, supply still shows a low level of concentration and poor capacity to offer logistics services that go beyond transport. Though Italy has, in recent years, recovered its key role on the international 'chessboard' of transport and logistics, the position of Italian firms both on domestic and international markets remains weak.

Logistics and transport service firms suffer mainly from the structural weakness of the Italian transport system in terms of level of infrastructure, scarce planning capacity of public operators, entrepreneurial capacity and logistics know-how. This has brought about a supply from many firms which are often sub-critical in size and dependent on a few historical customers.

Specifically, the supply is very highly structured: about 154,000 firms, with 411,000 employees, are involved in the field of logistics and freight transport (Confetra, 1999a). Road transport firms (145,000) have the largest share (94%); the vast majority of these firms (86.5%) are small, with an average of 2.1 employees per firm. The larger firms operate in the handling sector (forwarders included), with 29.4 employees, while the logistics operators lie in between with about 7 employees (Table 4.4).

Table 4.4 Structure of the Italian logistics and transport market

	Number of firms	Number of employees	Employees per firm
Haulage Firms	145,000	304,087	2.1
Logistics Operators	7,000	50,445	7.2
Handling	1,918	56,363	29.4

Source: CONFETRA, 1999a

In-depth analysis of the structure of road transport firms shows the following: 76.1% of firms have 1 employee, 11.1% have 2 employees and 94.7% have no more than 5 employees (Confetra, 1999b). This has created a widespread phenomenon in road transport: the transport subcontract. High labour costs and the huge investments required to supply a wide range of road transport services have led medium-large road transport firms to outsource part of their transport logistics by means of informal partnerships with small hauliers. They can thus minimise total costs while ensuring high quality service, in terms of reliability, speed, regularity and safety.

Hence a large number of small hauliers operate directly for medium-large hauliers, supplying transport services at the local or regional level (Confetra, 1999a).

With reference to maritime transport, the Italian shipping market also has a large number of small and medium shipping firms, mainly operating in dry bulk and liquid bulk sectors, as well as an entrepreneurial mentality loath to accept change, and thus very often unprepared to face an increasingly complex competitive environment (Evangelista, Morvillo, 2000).

In this scenario, it is difficult for logistics and transport operators to succeed in generating the financial resources required to expand both on the domestic and overseas market. In Italian firms, far-reaching cultural, structural and organisational changes, together with a suitable business size are required (Federtrasporto, 1999).

This situation is basically the result of a transport policy which focuses on the preservation of employment levels and protection of firms from international competition.

The belated liberalisation of the maritime and port sector has not given rise to a port-market logistics system that is capable of ensuring a functional link between ports and demand-generating centres.

In recent years, the globalisation of the market, the reducing of government interface, the continuing improvement of technologies and the renewed central role played by Italy in the Mediterranean area, has generated increasing interest from foreign operators both in strategically important ports (where the main container port-terminals belong to large international operators) and in logistics services and road transport (where a substantial number of national leaders operate in partnership with foreign operators).

The increased presence of foreign capital investment on the Italian market can also be attributed to the capacity of large international groups to exploit the cultural and financial weakness of Italian firms in maintaining the growth processes required to ward off competition.

This has led to a radical restructuring and concentrating process in the transport sector, and especially in shipping, where the development strategies of foreign firms, aimed at gaining control of the network of freight flows, have led to increasing numbers of acquisitions and mergers (Table 4.5).

Table 4.5 Mergers and acquisitions in the Italian logistics and transport market (1988-1998*)

	Logistics and road transport	Maritime transport (a)	Air transport (b)	Other	Total
Italian operations abroad	13	11	3	9	36
Foreign operations in Italy	43	17	6	12	78
Balance	−30	−6	−3	−3	−42

* Until 30 March 1999
(a) Port activities included
(b) Air activities included

Source: Federtrasporto 1999

Foreign firms are leaders in all segments of the Italian logistics and transport market. The balance between Italian operations abroad and foreign operations in Italy is negative in every segment, while logistics and road transport have experienced many more mergers and acquisitions. In shipping, acquisitions have chiefly involved container terminals, especially in transhipment ports. By contrast, significant operations are not recorded on international markets by Italian firms, a further sign of their economic, financial and competitive weakness compared with foreign operators. Hence, in order to meet the market's requirements and to compete internationally, Italian firms should (Merlino, Testa, Valivano, 1997):

♦ manage organically the various stages of the transport chain by supplying door-to-door services;
♦ acquire specialised skills that can broaden and diversify activities with higher value-added services on the basis of customer needs;
♦ realise key investments in physical infrastructure and ICT (Information and Communication Technology) , required for the provision of complex services;
♦ develop organisational agreements with other operators in the logistics chain.

In such a dynamic environment, development opportunities for Italian firms are thus strictly dependent on their ability to reorganise logistics and transport activities, by focussing on specific customer requirements and thereby achieving specialisation in particular market niches.

The Analysis of Logistics and Transport Operators in Campania

The previously highlighted charcteristics of the Italian logistics and transport market have stressed the wide competitive gap between Italian firms and foreign operators in structural, cultural and operational terms.

The analysis conducted at the regional level aims to highlight the peculiarities of the 'logistics and transport' market in Campania, which has a large number of small and medium firms and a heavily fragmented transport system, unable to guarantee an effective link between the different phases of the supply chain.

Methodology

Due to the lack of homogeneous sources, a database of logistics and freight transport operators needed to be set up initially. To this aim, the following sources were chosen:

♦ Ruote d'Italia and Tuttotrasporti (Italian specialised journals) for road haulage firms and Campania port data;
♦ Portnet[2] (Italian maritime portal) and Transport[3] (web site) for other operators (Table 4.6).

On the basis of geographical location and business activity, the sample consisted in 200 firms: 60 road transport firms and 140 other operators such as forwarders and shipping agencies (70), shipping firms (64) and terminal operators (6).

Table 4.6 Structure of the sample

Transport and logistics operator	Number of firms in Campania (a)	Number of firms interviewed (b)	% sample out of total (b/a)
Road transport firms	1872	60	3.2%
Forwarders and shipping agencies	214	70	32.7%
Shipping firms	307	64	20.8%
Terminal operators	10	6	60.0%
Total	**2403**	**200**	**8.3%**

The sampling for the different operators was defined on the basis of the variability of business activity; due to their homogeneity, the road transport firms were limited to 2.5% of the total number of firms in Campania.

The questionnaire was structured into two parts: the first focussed on general information of the business size of logistics and transport operators (i.e., numbers of employees and vehicles); the second specifically focussed on the peculiarities of logistics and transport service supply.

The aim of the survey was to identify the characteristics of the different operators according to the following variables:

♦ *Business scope.*
Evaluation of the differentiation degree of logistics and transport services was developed by identifying the different types of logistics services supplied. The questionnaire proposed a classification of logistics services, with an increasingly complex degree, asking operators to specify the services they supply directly and those through sub-contracting, agreements, alliances, etc, with other operators;[4]
♦ *Relationships with other logistics and transport operators.*
Relationships were divided into horizontal (between operators that supply the same services) and vertical agreements (between operators that supply different services along the logistics chain);
♦ *Percentage of investments in logistics and transport facilities.*

Air transport was not analysed in this survey, as it accounts for only a small share in the Campania logistics and freight transport market.

The Empirical Results

Road Transport Firms in Campania

As the road transport firms are widely located all over Campania, some distribution rates both at regional (ratio of firms located in the provinces to the total in Campania) and provincial levels (ratio of firms located in each city to the provincial total) were created to give more significance to the sampling (Table 4.7).

Table 4.7 Distribution of road transport firms in Campania

Cities	Road Transport Firms in the Provinces		Road Transport Firms City/Province	
	No. of firms in each province	*% of Campania total*	*No. of firms in the city*	*% of provincial total*
Avellino	136	7.3%	10	7.4%
Benevento	229	12.2%	51	22.3%
Caserta	473	25.3%	25	5.3%
Naples	491	26.2%	141	28.7%
Salerno	543	29.0%	52	9.6%
Total	**1872**	**100.0%**	**279**	**15.0%**

Source: Our processing on Ruote d'Italia data – 1998

In fact, road transport firms show different patterns according to their proximity to strategic distribution centres or traffic nodes (like Salerno and Naples ports) and the specialisation of demand (like Caserta).

Figure 4.1 shows the results of the survey according to two variables: investments in logistics activities and relationships with other logistics and transport operators. The business scope of road transport firms was limited, above all, to transport; therefore it did not represent a critical variable of the analysis.[5] The bubble size indicates the number of firms (*frequency*) that have the same level of investment in logistics activities and the same typology of relationships.

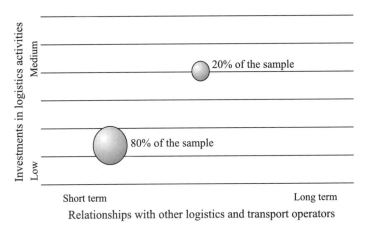

Figure 4.1 Road transport in Campania: the empirical survey

The majority of the firms interviewed are positioned on the left side of the diagram, with short-term relationships and a low interest in logistics activity.

The relationships are basically horizontal agreements, i.e. with other road transport firms, while vertical agreements are less developed. This is a consequence of the business size of road haulage firms (small and medium size) and the competitive environment (regional and national markets) in which they operate. Moreover, the need to develop a flexible organisational structure and to guarantee widespread distribution has led the large road transport firms to outsource part of the transport to small hauliers. In general, agreements between large road transport firms and small hauliers are *informal* and *short-term* and so their positioning is on the left side of the figure.

By contrast, vertical agreements (i.e. between the logistics chain operators) are concluded when transport demand is regular and transport operators orientate their strategic choices towards the supply of door-to-door services. Only a few road transport firms interviewed (generally large firms with foreign capital) formally conclude vertical agreements: these firms are positioned on the right side of the figure.

The low development of relationships in the supply of logistics services is also correlated to low levels of investment in other activities beyond transport. The majority of these have only invested in vehicles, while a very low percentage (20% of firms interviewed, represented mainly by medium-large firms) has invested in information systems and logistics infrastructure (i.e., warehouses and depots).

Figure 4.1, therefore, shows two groups of firms. The larger, representative of

80% of the road transport firms interviewed, indicates a short-term relationship with other operators and low investment in logistics; they are small in size, with an average of 2 employees and 1 lorry and they generally supply transport services in local or regional areas.

The smaller group, 20% of the sample, shows a more dynamic positioning in the market; they are mainly road transport firms of medium and large size with an average of 40 employees and 30 lorries, supplying transport services for national markets. More specifically, these firms are particularly skilled in the supply of specialised transport services which take into account freight characteristics and customer requirements. The presence of specialised production areas (such as the Agro-Nocerino Sarnese and Solofra[6]) has led to the concentration and specialisation of transport services. Such areas, therefore, represent potential demand for logistics and transport services.

From the survey it has been possible to delineate the characteristics of the supply of logistics services in the Agro-Nocerino Sarnese and Solofra areas.

The *Agro-Nocerino Sarnese* area, with its production of perishable goods (vegetables, fruits and food preserves), has developed a niche market, in which road transport firms are strictly dependent on the producer's requirements. The small hauliers distribute the end products locally, on the basis of informal agreements with producers. In other words, there is no steady relationship between the demand and supply of logistics and transport services.

Large road hauliers supply transport services over long distances to distribution centres in northern Italy.

The location near the production area has great strategic importance, since road transport firms can satisfy the *just-in-time* requirements of producers. Moreover, large road hauliers invest in specific structures for food storage and transport (refrigerated lorries), supplying other logistics services, such as freight warehousing and storage, quality control and loading.

The port of Salerno and, to a lesser extent, Naples represent the main traffic hubs for national distribution (short sea shipping) while, for international transport, freight is generally transported to the port of Gioia Tauro by feeder services.

The *Solofra area* is characterised by a large number of tanneries. Transport services are dominated by a few large road hauliers which, through a price-agreement, regulate transport relationships towards the distribution centres of central-northern Italy (Florence and Vicenza). Horizontal agreements allow the road transport firms to regain competitiveness by charging a higher price for distribution to end-users. In international traffic, local producers delegate the forwarder to manage and organise transport and logistics activities.

The Maritime Transport Sector

The analysis presented in this section starts from the consideration that maritime transport generally involves different operators, such as shipping firms (diversified in the main shipping areas: dry and liquid bulk, general cargo and container), small and medium size shipping firms (specialised in specific niche market), shipping agents and forwarders (that organise the transport chain on behalf of their customers) and terminal operators.

The sample was selected after setting up a general database of the different shipping operators. Table 4.8 shows the aggregation of operators according to their geographical location in the ports of Naples and Salerno, regardless of the nature and conditioning of the goods transported.

The sample consisted of the following: 140 operators, of whom 50% were shipping agents and forwarders, 40% shipping firms and 5% terminal operators.

The multifunctional characteristic of the port of Naples and the heterogeneity of its freight traffic led to the extrapolation of a larger number of operators, about 70% of the representative sample.

By contrast, the port of Salerno is highly specialised in freight traffic and has a large concentration of the supply of transport services; the operators interviewed formed 30% of the sample. Subsequently, three large strategic areas of activity were identified which are consistent with the aims of the present work: liquid and dry bulk, break-bulk and container and Ro/Ro.

Table 4.8 Maritime transport operators in Campania

	Port of Naples	**Port of Salerno**
Shipping agent	83	19
Shipping firm	222	85
Terminal operator	7	3
Forwarder	74	38
Total	**386**	**145**

Source: Portnet and Campania and Livorno port data, 1999

Liquid and Dry Bulk

In the liquid bulk segment, where the main actor is the manufacturing industry or the forwarder that sees to the shipment of the goods, competitive pressure is lower and the choice of the port terminal is generally dependent on the location of the production facilities.

The terminals were left out of the survey because they are generally managed directly by manufacturing industries. Moreover, the major industrial groups (iron, steel, oil industries, etc.) tend to control transport activities through the ownership of vessels or through stable relationships with shipping companies. Thus, the liquid and dry bulk segments constitute a very concentrated supply, while logistics integration has been promoted by firms which have their roots in the trading sector.

In the port of Salerno, this segment lies beyond the interest of logistics and transport operators, who have gradually directed investments to specific niche markets (Ro/Ro, car and perishable goods).

In the port of Naples, although bulk traffic was a profitable segment, the lack of a port policy oriented to the development and specialisation of the infrastructure per specific market segment has led to a shift of this traffic to other ports.

Therefore, shipping companies in liquid and dry bulk are small in size, supplying transport services only in Italy (cabotage), especially to Sicily and Sardinia; most of the sample (about 90%) does not supply services other than transport.

Break-bulk

Break-bulk cargo usually consists of semi-finished and finished products, wood and other products differing greatly in value and transport modes. The main tendency of this segment of the market has been the progressive specialisation of suprastructures on the basis of specific characteristics of goods, such as warehouses and depots for the preservation of forest products.

In the port of Salerno, the Gallozzi group manages the transport chain of wood by supplying maritime and road transport services, and the handling of cargoes in the Salerno Container Terminal. The organisation of services is based on stable relationships with other operators.

In the port of Naples, on the other hand, information obtained from the questionnaires highlighted the following peculiarities:

♦ 80% of the shipping firms interviewed are small in size and supply transport services within the national market (cabotage) and Mediterranean area (short sea shipping);
♦ The entire sample prefers to have short-term agreements with maritime agents and freight forwarders;
♦ The terminals are multipurpose, i.e. they combine container and Ro/Ro handling activities. In the port of Naples, SO.TE.CO. operates in partnership with Ignazio Messina, and it manages a considerable proportion of wood traffic;
♦ 90% of the forwarders and maritime agents diversified supply on the basis of specific customer requirements, mainly organising maritime and road transport and freight warehousing and storage.

International Liner Shipping

Analysis of the characteristics of operators in international liner transport is more complex because the shipping sector has undergone profound changes, mainly represented by the development strategies of large international groups (oriented to integration of the different stages of the transport chain). Within this changing context, the most significant Italian groups operating in international liner services have been analysed. Focusing chiefly on the shipping phase of transport, it is apparent that some Italian operators (such as Grimaldi Group, Naples) have pursued a strategy of growth by acquisition, thus achieving a better competitive position in niche markets.

By contrast, other firms (such as Clerici Logistic Group) have shifted their attention from a *port-to-port* approach to that of *door-to-door*, so as to provide a service which better suits customer needs.

The ports of Naples and Salerno, although neighbouring, perform differently in the field of container traffic (% container/total freight traffic), as the table below shows.

Table 4.9 Total freight and containers in the ports of Salerno and Naples – 1998

Ports	Total freight	Containers	Containers/ Total freight
Salerno	5.309.705	2.516.438	**47.39%**
Naples	14.777.067	3.103.595	**21.00%**

Source: Ministry of Transport and Navigation, 1999

Container traffic in the port of Salerno accounts for 47% of the total freight, while in the port of Naples it represents only 21%. This is a consequence of different policies adopted by the two ports: the specialisation of Salerno underlines a different supply structure compared with Naples.

The results of the survey show a different competitive positioning between the operators of the ports of Naples and those of Salerno.

In the port of Naples there are some foreign liner shipping firms (such as Coscos) that were left out of the survey and a large number of small Italian shipping firms operating in short sea shipping, which are poorly integrated in the logistics chain. In fact, 70% of the sample claim to have close relationships only with maritime agents and freight forwarders.

One of the main Italian operators is Ignazio Messina & Co. that offers maritime services in containers, Ro/Ro, cars and forest products. As freight rates are continuously going down, the transport of different cargoes by multipurpose vessels enables the company to be competitive in certain niche markets, mainly in its Mediterranean relations.[7] The company can be defined as an *intermodal operator* because, besides shipping services in the strict sense, it supplies port terminal management, groupage and unit loading services, and land transport by rail (Evangelista, Morvillo, 2000). The transport chain is controlled through its close relationship with the maritime agent, Morelli, which is located close to the port of Naples. This agent has an important financial stake in the SO.TE.CO. terminal.

In the port of Salerno, however, shipping firms have a high degree of specialisation in niche markets (Ro/Ro, cars and perishable goods). In the case of Grimaldi Group, Naples, the segment of the transport of new cars is an interesting example of innovation in business differentiation achieved by supplying logistics services other than transport.

The Grimaldi Group of Naples manages the traffic in new cars and Ro/Ro through the Salerno Container Terminal. Salerno is the main port of the Grimaldi multipurpose Euro Med Service, linking Salerno to 17 ports in the Mediterranean and European area. On the basis of long-term agreements with its customers (Fiat and Ford, Opel, Peugeot, Renault, Seat), the Group supplies intermodal transport along with a set of value-added services, including warehousing, waxing and dewaxing of cars. Over the last few years, Grimaldi has made substantial investments in terminals and new vessels (i.e., car carriers), improving the quality of its services, and has established alliances with national and international partners, thereby activating an integration process of sea and hinterland transport.

Terminal Operators

The terminals, as previously described, have been the target of a large number of acquisitions and mergers by national and foreign shipping firms. In fact, the strategic choice aiming to achieve control of the whole transport chain has led the shipping line to take over the management of port terminals either directly or by acquiring firms already performing in the industry.

The analysis starts with a description of the companies' organisational structure in the port of Naples:

♦ SO.TE.CO., a terminal specialised in containers, Ro/Ro and general cargo handling, is controlled by Navarmar (98% of share capital), a company belonging to the Morelli maritime agency. The Morelli Agency manages the Ro/Ro and container traffic on behalf of the Ignazio Messina shipping company, through long-term agreements;

♦ CO.NA.TE.CO. is a merger of three terminal operators: Fariello&Luise S.r.l. (40% of share capital), Luigi Ievoli S.r.l. (40%) and D'Orazio S.r.l. (20%). The terminal supplies container handling services for a large number of international shipping firms, in particular for CosCos (a joint venture between Cosco and Cosulich);

♦ Flavio Gioia Terminal (TFG), is controlled by Cargo Service (83%) a company belonging to the Bucci Shipping Agency. Recently, TFG reached an agreement with CO.NA.TE.CO., aiming to upgrade the level of service to be offered and guaranteed to the shipping lines already calling in Naples. The Bucci Shipping Agency also possesses share capital in the Salerno Container Terminal.

The terminal characteristics in the port of Salerno are as follows:

♦ Salerno Container Terminal is managed chiefly by the Gallozzi Group and Contship (25%). The Gallozzi Group handles 70% of the container traffic of the port of Salerno. The Group acts as agent for large shipping firms, like Maersk, Sea Land, Grand Alliance, P&O NL (Australia and New Zealand service), Hanjin, Zim, Lloyd Triestino and Italia di Navigazione-MPE;

♦ Salerno Auto Terminal, controlled by Michele Autori (50%), a firm in the Grimaldi Group of Naples.

The main feature of terminal operators in the port of Naples is their functional autonomy in the supply of handling services. This means that the operators are chiefly involved in maritime business, without the specialisation required to ensure the satisfaction of homogeneous logistics needs.

Conversely, in the port of Salerno, the terminals are dedicated to (i.e., they are exclusively controlled by a limited number of operators) and specialised in the handling and storage of containers, Ro/Ro and perishable goods. In particular, the Clerici Logistic Group is the Italian leader in the logistics of perishables. The Group directly manages specialised terminals in the ports of Salerno, Genoa, Ravenna and Trieste, through a series of operative firms. Besides specialised inter-modal transport services, all logistics activities are performed, ranging from health and safety controls to the quality control of goods.

Shipping Agents and Forwarders[8]

As part of the survey, interviews were conducted with approximately 70 businesses of varying size. Of these, 70% had a simple structure, averaging 3 employees, whereas 30% were medium in size, with more than 40 employees.

A common feature of all the operators interviewed, regardless of their business size or location, was their respective specialisation in market niches. This arose not only from their difficulty to remain competitive at the international level, but also because it provided a means to maximise opportunities offered by specific segments of the market. Indeed, 90% of the operators interviewed specified that they generally organise the transport chain on the basis of customer requirements.

Substantial differences, however, were found insofar as business sized was concerned and agreements with other operators in the logistics chain. Small-scale operators are active at the national level and are chiefly involved at the shipping stage and transport through informal co-operative relations with local firms.

Medium-sized enterprises, on the other hand, also operate at the international level, chiefly through co-operative relations with shipping companies and road haulage firms; 20% of these enterprises offer transport and logistics services through foreign partners and subsidiaries. Since port efficiency plays a fundamental role in the competitiveness of forwarders and shipping agents, further differences emerged from the interviews conducted with operators in the ports of Salerno and Naples.

In the port of Salerno, there are fewer large maritime agents and forwarders with a higher level of specialisation and integration within the logistics chain. On the shipping leg, maritime agents and forwarders offer maritime transport services on the basis of long-term agreements with shipping firms, while road transport is managed through co-operative relations with road transport firms.

By contrast, in Naples there are more than 300 operators, few of which are large, such as Fratelli Trimarco, Hugo Trumpy, Le Navi and P. Scerni S.p.a., Cargo Service (Portnet, 2000). Intermediation is thus performed by a large number of operators in relation to transport demand. This is one of the main causes of the fragmentation of the transport chain, constantly characterised by the heterogeneous control and management of its services. The lack of co-ordination between the stages of the logistics chain generates widespread inefficiency in supplying logistics and transport services, and has thus led to the marginal position of operators in Campania, in national and international terms.

Conclusions

The aim of this work has been to outline the characteristics of logistics and transport operators in southern Italy, in the light of the changes affecting a) the production system, oriented to outsourcing a considerable amount of the manufacturing process and b) the transport sector, driven in the direction of concentration and integration of transport activities upstream and downstream of the logistics chain. The survey showed that the supply of logistics and transport services in Campania experiences, for different reasons, broad regional dispersal, thereby favouring the growth of road transport. In each category analysed, partnerships seem to be less developed, preferring short and informal agreements.

With regard to maritime transport, the successful cases presented in this study refer to firms which have used a differentiation strategy through the supply of value-added logistics services. Our analysis has shown that few Italian shipping companies have achieved progressive expansion in their maritime business in their efforts to gain control of increasingly significant parts of the customer's logistics chain. The other shipping firms hold a very weak position in the international context and so have remained extraneous to developments under way.

Forwarders and maritime agents play a critical role in the supply chain because they organise and manage the system of relations between shipping companies, road transport firms and the end-consumer. Business size is important in co-operative relations with other operators in the transport chain. While the practice of vertical co-operative relations has spread in line with shipping firms and road transport firms, the provision of further logistics services is generally restricted to short-term relations and organised according to customer requirements.

Notes

1   The industrial district is a system of Italian SMEs specialised in one or more stages of the production process, with a high degree of inter-firm integration, and it is characterised by a sound tendency towards internationalisation.
2   http://www. portnet.it
3   http://www.transports.it
4   The logistics activities were divided into:
    *   Transport activities: maritime, road and railway transport;
    *   Inter-modal transport: road-rail, sea-road, Ro/Ro services;
    *   Warehouse, storage, product collection and loading;
    *   Freight transport clearance, loading and unloading services, import/export invoicing management;
    *   Other logistics services: quality control, packaging, labelling, pricing, etc.
5   The Campania market, as well as the Italian market, is characterised by transport cost competitiveness, with little development of logistics activities. Indeed, in response to the question *'What services do you supply beyond transport?'*, most road transport firms specified that the lack of regular transport demand does not allow them to invest in other logistics activities (such as freight warehousing and storage, product collection and loading). Only 10% of road transport firms supply other than logistics services (typically warehousing); they tend to be large businesses with considerable transport demand in quantitative terms.
6   These areas usually contain a substantial concentration of firms specialised in one or more stages of the same production process and operating in conditions of high inter-firm integration.
7   Direct services are supplied in 'short' distance connections, e.g. between Naples and other Mediterranean ports.
8   For the purposes of this study, shipping agents and forwarders were considered as a single category; although they carried out diverse activities in the past (the former acting directly on behalf of ship owners, and the latter representing the shippers), they now offer the same logistics services besides transport.

References

Bhatnagar, R., and Viswanathan, S. (2000), 'Re-engineering global supply chains. Alliances between manufacturing and global logistics services providers', *International Journal of Physical Distribution & Logistics Management*, Vol. 30, no. 1, 2000, MCB University Press.

Bologna, S. (1997), 'Una logistica per i distretti industriali', *Logistica Management*, (74), 53-62.

Bowersox, D.J., and Closs, D.J. (1996), *Logistical management: The Integrated Supply Chain Process*, McGraw-Hill, New York.

CENSIS (1998), 'Logistica e trasporti: soggetti e processi per la competitività del Sistema-Paese', *Studi e ricerche*, Gangemi Editore.

CONFETRA (1999a), 'Il mercato Italia dei servizi logistici e di trasporto negli anni '90', Quaderno n°112.

CONFETRA (1999b), 'Profilo dell'autotrasporto di cose in Italia', Quaderno no. 87/3, Conto Nazionale dei Trasporti 1999.

CSST (1997), 'Prospettive del trasporto merci a medio e lungo termine in Italia', *Centro Studi sui Sistemi di Trasporto*.

Davis, T. (1993), 'Effective supply chain management', *Sloan Management Review*, Summer.

Evangelista, P., Morvillo, A. (2000), 'Maritime Transport in the Italian Logistics Market', *Maritime Policy and Management*, Vol. 27, no. 4, October - December.

Federtrasporto (2000), 'L'internazionalizzazione del trasporto: la posizione dell'impresa italiana', *Bollettino Economico sui trasporti*, no. 10.

Gruppo CLAS (1998), 'The fundamental variables which affect decisions concerning intermodal transport', *Project funded by European Commission under the Transport RTD Programme of the 4th Framework Programme*.

Maggi, E. (1998), 'Terziarizzazione: una nuova opportunità di crescita per le imprese di trasporto', *Trasporti Europei*.

Maltz, A.B., and Ellram, L.M. (1997), 'Total cost relationship: an analytical framework for the logistics outsourcing decisions', *Journal of Business Logistics*, Vol. 18, no. 1.

MarketLine International (1997), *EU Logistics*.

Merlino, M., Testa, T. and Valivano, A. (1997), 'Opportunità e limiti dei processi di outsourcing. Esperienze della logistica', *Economia & Management*, no. 3, May 1997.

Montella, B. (1999), 'Il ruolo del porto di Napoli nello sviluppo del traffico merci nel Mediterraneo', *Trasporti Europei*.

Paci, G. (2000), 'Special Report', *Lloyd's List*.

Quaderni del PGT (1999), *Politiche per la logistica e il trasporto merci. Logistica ed intermodalità*, no. 3/99.

Razzaque M, .A., and Sheng, C.C. (1998), 'Outsourcing of logistics functions: a literature survey', *International Journal of Physical Distribution & Logistics Management*, Vol. 28, no. 2, 1998, MCB University Press.

Skjoett-Larsen, T. (2000), ' Third party logistics - from an interorganizational point of view', *International Journal of Physical Distribution & Logistics Management*, Vol. 30, no. 2, 2000, MCB University Press.

Stank, P., and Goldsby, T.F. (2000), 'A framework for transportation decision making in an integrated supply chain', *Supply Chain Management: An International Journal*, Vol. 5, no. 2, 2000, MCB University Press.

Chapter 5

Entrepreneurial Culture in Logistics and Freight Transport: Cross-industry and Cross-country Analysis

Antonio Minguzzi and Alfonso Morvillo

Recent Developments in the Freight Transport Industry in Italy

In recent decades the freight transport industry has developed along increasingly complex lines, due in particular to the rapid introduction of new information technologies. This phenomenon is triggering organisational and relational restructuring among business actors, which has given rise to a new vision of all activities as parts of a single chain: the logistical chain. Moreover, the growing internationalisation of logistical and transport activities has contributed to making the economic environment more complex and competitive.

In this scenario, information technology and telecommunications assume strategic importance in relation to direct horizontal competition between competing firms and vertical competition within the industry.

In Italy, both country-specific and industry-specific factors have affected the development of the transport industry in recent years. In relation to country-specific factors, a negative role has been played by fragmented or even absent planning to develop infrastructures, which has not properly considered the modal integration dynamics of transport. A significant role has also been played by the particular structure of the production and distribution system, chiefly based on small and medium enterprises. Such circumstances taken as a whole have not given the firms operating in the transport chain the necessary external stimuli to implement the leap in quality in supplying a service based on the growing use of information technology and telecommunications.

During the last few years, a series of structural changes connected with changes in the national regulatory framework, completion of the European integration process and the growing interest of foreign firms in the Italian market of logistical and transport services, have reduced the role of *country-specific* factors.

By contrast, in relation to *firm-specific* factors the freight transport industry, especially in southern Italy, is characterised by an entrepreneurial culture which reflects the artisanal spirit of the many small firms operating there. Strictly connected with this aspect, the development strategies of most of the national transport firms focus on short-term objectives whereas they should have been addressed towards developing synergies and competitive advantages based on the

75

reduction of transaction costs and the increase in customer satisfaction level (Evangelista, Morvillo, 1998).

Moreover, it is well known that the small and medium size of operators gives rise to a series of constraints and limitations to business development pathways. Their evolution is dependent on the characteristics of the entrepreneur's own culture which affects his/her competitiveness both in the short and long term.

The aim of this paper is to analyse, through an empirical survey, the relations between entrepreneurial own culture and the introduction of Information and Communication Technology (ICT) in small freight transport firms in southern Italy (Campania). The background of relevant literature is first explored so as to illustrate the model used to analyse entrepreneurship and the method employed to detect the relationship between entrepreneurship and ICT. Lastly, after outlining the results of the empirical survey, certain implications are evaluated for smaller firms and public policy.

The Role of Entrepreneurial Culture in the Smaller Firm

The entrepreneurial culture prevalent in southern Italian SMEs of the traditional industries plays a *critical role* in implementing or impeding business change and evolution (Minguzzi, Passaro, 1997; Evangelista, Morvillo, 1998). Generally, small entrepreneurs tackle change *culturally* by often trying to resist it, thereby creating a constraint to the exchange of knowledge which drives each firm's necessary evolution in time. Indeed, this acts as a barrier to individual and collective learning processes and hence to the development paths required to maintain and improve a firm's competitiveness. Moreover, in specialised areas this tends to create a homogeneous culture among firms due to similar educational, social and professional backgrounds experienced by the entrepreneurs (MacGrath *et al.* 1992). However, if in such situations the entrepreneurs are *willing to change*, innovations tend to be passed on rapidly among all the sectoral operators, allowing *followers* who behave imitatively to take advantage of the new techniques developed by the *leaders*.

The role of entrepreneurial culture is important in that it affects relational learning processes which firms implement with the economic environment that surrounds them. Entrepreneurial culture consists of values, propensities and behaviour which characterise the entrepreneur in terms of his/her spirit of initiative, propensity to risk and innovative capacity (Schumpeter, 1934; Slevin, Covin, 1990). For the purposes of this paper the entrepreneur is the person able to modify the structure of relations between the firm and the economic environment through the characteristics of the entrepreneurial culture. The latter, in turn, is modified by learning processes that enhance a firm's competitiveness by developing the entrepreneur's managerial and cognitive skills (Hendry, Hope, 1994).

This highlights the complex, heterogeneous nature of the issue which still lacks general theorising. In research terms, studies of entrepreneurship aim to *comprehend* and *predict* the entrepreneur's actions to evaluate their success or failure in relation to certain stimuli from the external economic *environment* (Minguzzi, Passaro, 2000). Indeed, this creates favourable conditions for the development of the entrepreneurial culture and hence economic development.

The most recent scientific contributions highlight a pathway that starts from the *individual* (entrepreneur) and connects with his/her *actions* within a changing *economic environment*. It should be assumed that the entrepreneur is not an actor who automatically responds in set fashion to the stimuli of the external environment but is instead capable of learning, creating and thus affecting the economic environment from which he/she receives stimuli. There is thus the risk of generating a paradox constructed on the difficulty of inserting within a deterministic and predictable approach the entrepreneur's dynamic behaviour aiming to create innovation. According to this approach, the entrepreneur's role as a creator of innovation may thus be represented as:

$$\text{individual (I)} = \text{new value creation (NVC)}$$

which constitutes a *dialogic* system, that is, with non-unidirectional circular causality.

Using a similar approach Filion (1998) identifies the contribution of entrepreneurial action as being useful for the development of the economic system when:

$$(L+CR)\ I > C$$

where
L   =   learning
CR =   creative
I   =   implementation
C   =   rate of change

Thus the learning parameter is identified as underlying the innovation, although it is connected dynamically to the transformation of entrepreneurial *skills* into innovation only when its practical implementation generates 'topical' novelties ahead of the *rate of change*.

In recent years the role of learning in developing competitive strategies of success has been highlighted in the literature (Argyris, Schon, 1978; Schein, 1984, 1992; Smith, Peterson, 1988; Huber, 1991; Sackmann, 1991; Kotter, Heskett, 1992; Garvin, 1993), especially because the phenomenon assumes an essential role in development processes especially in smaller firms (Nonaka 1997; Minguzzi, Passaro, 2000).

The approaches illustrated show that the theme embraces different aspects of the economic sciences, from those concerning areas to those more strictly concerning firms. Indeed, the framework for the study of the *determinants* of the formation processes of entrepreneurship is *firm-specific* (Bull, Willard, 1993; Bygrave, 1993), *industry-specific* (McDougall, 1989) and *country-specific* (Hofstede, 1994) which are combined in each situation with different equilibria (Minguzzi, Passaro, 1997).

The Structure of Empirical Analysis

Based on such considerations, the issue of empirical analysis of entrepreneurial profiles has already been tackled by an approach which considered *simultaneously* the three arrangements of determinants: *firm*, *industry* and *country* (Minguzzi, Morvillo, 2000). Retaining this approach, which aims to highlight the various roles and weights of the determinants of entrepreneurship, this work sets out to identify the link between the various entrepreneurial profiles emerging from the analysis and the issues related to the introduction of information technology in the 148 small firms observed.

Given the approach outlined above, the introduction of ICT in the freight transport industry is a function of three orders of factors, which may be represented by the following relation:

$$\Delta \text{ICT} = f(\text{CF, IF, FF})$$

where CF are *country factors*, IF *industrial factors* and FF *firm factors*.

On investigating the characteristics of individual factors, especially in relation to the specific nature of smaller firms, the *firm factors* are a function of the following variables:

$$FI = f(\text{firm structure, entrepreneurial culture})$$

where, in turn, *entrepreneurial culture* is a function of: the human profile of the entrepreneur, his/her behaviour and opinions. Accordingly Figure 5.1 shows the conceptual grid between the survey determinants and the variables gathered.

Figure 5.1 Conceptual matching determinants vs. variables of entrepreneurial profiles

		PROFILES		
		Entrepreneural behaviours	Firm's structures	IT Diffusion
DETERMINANTS	Country Factors	nationality		
	Industrial Factors		different industry in which the firm operates	
	Firm Factors	age of entrepreneur educational level years of experience firm's ownership foreign languages known delegation of responsibility trade association membership factor of success operative difficulties	legal form firm's age number of employees	hardware software internet difficulties of introducing IT benefit of introducing IT

Thus, in light of the above explanation, the statistical analysis performed was shown in Figure 5.2.

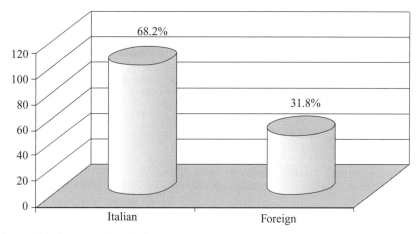

Figure 5.2 Model of statistical analysis

The Survey

The Questionnaire

The questionnaire was designed by making allowances both for the in-house skills of Institute for Service Industry Research with regard to entrepreneurial culture and ICT, and the indications emerging from interviews with Trade Associations involved as partners in the FIT project. The questionnaire consists of an initial section devoted to general information on the firm and two sections corresponding to specific aspects to be investigated, namely entrepreneurial culture and the level of diffusion of ICT in the firm.

The questions on the firm chiefly concern its structural aspects (legal form, number of employees) and the industry characteristics. The questions on culture regard both the entrepreneurial profile of the interviewee (origins, educational level, entreprenurial experience) and the established management practices in the firm (intensity and breadth of delegation of responsibility, openness towards the outside environment). Special attention is also focused on analysing the driving factors of success and the constraints to entrepreneurial action according to the entrepreneur's own perceptions.

The last part of the questionnaire concerns various aspects of ICT in the firm, with particular reference to the nature of both hardware and software used in the firm, their contribution and type of support supplied to the various company functions, and the way such systems are organised. Other questions also concern the difficulties in implementing ICT systems, any barriers to the introduction of ICT in the firm or the benefits that it has afforded.

Structural Characteristics of Firms

Prior to quantitative analysis, it is worth outlining some qualitative results on the data gathered by administering the questionnaires. The results are presented in relation to the frequency distributions of variables, both simple and double, which link the firm's structural aspects with variables explaining the entrepreneurial culture or the responses expressed by entrepreneurs on ICT.

The first variable considered is the nationality of the entrepreneur. As may be observed (Figure 5.3), the majority of interviewees (68%) are Italian, while the rest (32%) chiefly consist of Dutch entrepreneurs.

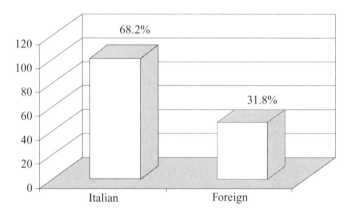

Figure 5.3 Sample distribution by nationality

With reference to the educational level, data analysis (Figure 5.4) shows that all the interviewees have a high school qualification; the most numerous group (about 57%) only has a high school diploma; other smaller but non-marginal groups have degrees (24%) or have done a post-high school specialisation (19%).

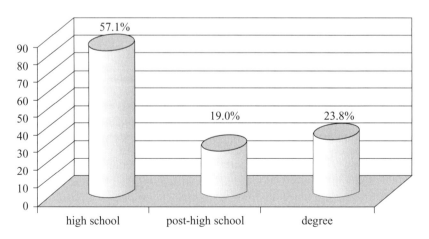

Figure 5.4 Distribution of interviewees by educational level

As regards age (Figure 5.5), the sample distribution is highly concentrated in the 36-54 age class, while the classes of young (<35 years old – 25%) and older entrepreneurs (>54 years old – 21%) have approximately the same weight.

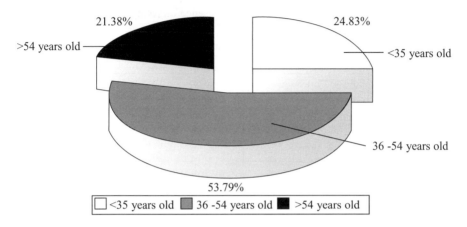

Figure 5.5 Distribution of interviewees by age of entrepreneurs

In terms of firm size (number of employees), the distribution of firms (Figure 5.6) shows a marked presence of micro-firms with fewer than 10 employees (56%). So-called small firms, with a number of employees between 10 and 49, are also significantly represented (approximately 32%), while medium-size firms with over 49 employees have a marginal weight (about 12%). Larger firms are completely absent.

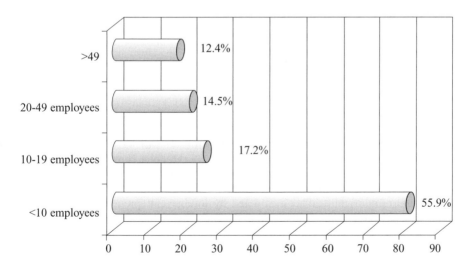

Figure 5.6 Firm size by number of employees

A further aspect of the sample considered is the start-up year. Analysis of the data (Figure 5.7) shows a considerable rootedness in the industry of firms examined. The firms that have operated for more than 10 years make up the majority of the sample (about 63%); of these, there is an appreciable proportion of firms established over 30 years ago (23%). There is also a substantial presence of younger firms (36% circa).

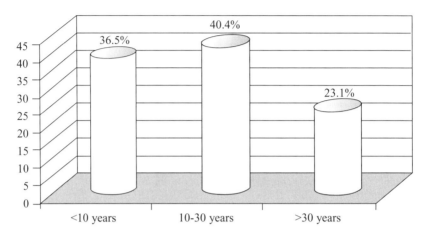

Figure 5.7 Distribution of firms by start-up year

Italian and foreign entrepreneurs, called to express a series of evaluations on the factors of success or impediments to the growth of entrepreneurial firms, gave somewhat differentiated results (Table 5.1). On factors underlying the firm's success the questionnaire distinguishes between those linked to the entrepreneur's personal qualities (innate or acquired factors) and those that are not a direct expression of entrepreneurial action (external factors). Foreign entrepreneurs show greater sensitivity to personal qualities (morality, rationality, intelligence) and, to a lesser extent, to external factors than their Italian counterparts; by contrast, Italian entrepreneurs attribute greater importance to factors linked to the acquisition of technical, economic and market knowledge (acquired factors).

With reference to operative difficulties, market variables (absence of entry barriers, shortage of demand, difficulty implementing forms of co-operation with competitors to achieve cost advantages) are considered more significant by foreign entrepreneurs; while with reference to environmental variables (lack of services, lack of facilities, environmental constraints, etc.), the latter show a relatively more significant preference. On in-house variables (personnel management, etc.) the opinion of the two groups is basically identical.

The most significant difficulties noted by foreign entrepreneurs as regards the introduction of ICT in the firm concern: data confidentiality (52.17%), staff training (50%), and financial resources required for investments (42.55%). The majority of Italian entrepreneurs report no significant difficulties in this sense, except in relation to training (43.33%).

The benefits of introducing ICT are perceived by the overwhelming majority of entrepreneurs of both groups observed. There is especially marked consistency in the responses supplied by foreign entrepreneurs: each alternative was chosen by over 72% of the interviewees. Italian entrepreneurs, however, showed greater variability in opinions: with reference to the positive effects on the service level there was almost total consensus (93.81%), while a much lower percentage rates the effects on competitiveness positively (48.42).

Overall, most of the entrepreneurs (67.13%) reported a high level of ICT diffusion in their firms and only a marginal percentage (10.49%) reported a total lack of ICT tools (Table 5.2) The most ICT-sensitive entrepreneurs seem to be young (under 35) and more mature (over 54). The proportion in these age groups of those who reported a high level of ICT (respectively 26.4% and 23.96%) is higher than their respective weight in the sample (respectively 24.48% and 20.98%). Finally, of those who reported that they did not use any ICT tools, the absolute majority (73.33) belongs to the 35-54 age class.

Findings

Multiple Correlation Analysis

Overall, the information obtained from the questionnaire produced a matrix with the firms interviewed in line and the variables corresponding to the questionnaire responses in columns, which was subjected to Multiple Correlation Analysis (MCA).[1] To this end the variables were classified into *active* and *illustrative*. The former, representing country variables, the firm's structure and the entrepreneurial culture (Table 5.3), were used to determine new factors; the latter, representing information technology and industry variables (Table 5.4), were only subsequently projected onto factorial plans.

This choice was made necessary by the large number of variables which would have excessively reduced the variability explained by each factor deriving from MCA. The solution adopted combines the required level of in-depth analysis with the survey's methodological needs.

The rule followed for choosing the best subspace is based on the factors corresponding to the eigenvalues that highlight discontinuities in the diagram of the percentages of explained variability (Table 5.5). In the case of MCA, the variability explained by each factor is an excessively pessimistic measurement of their actual explanatory capacity due to the very large number of the initial sizes.

Various methods have been proposed to adjust such values and define more realistic and reliable variability percentages. Among these is the adjustment proposed by Benzécri who considers only the eigenvalues greater than the reciprocal of the number of active variables.[2] In relative terms, the importance of each factor is calculated as follows: the square of each eigenvalue is divided by the sum of the squares of the eigenvalues over the threshold above (Table 5.6).

In Figure 5.8 we report the representation of points (categories) in the first factorial plan, (defined by the first and second factor) which represents the largest part of variability in the cluster of points observed (about 45% overall).

Through joint evaluation of the of the factorial plan of active variables, absolute contributions and value test of the active points on the two axes (Table 5.7),[3] the following considerations may be developed.

The *first factorial axis* is explained by nationality of entrepreneur, the variables linked to certain structural variables of firms and, lastly, the variables indicating the perception of factors of success and the constraints to entrepreneurial activity. It contrasts two groups of firms: on one side (positive semi-axis) emerge chiefly foreign firms established at least ten years before; on the other (negative semi-axis) are Italian firms which have operated for longer on the transport services market (more than ten years and, in some cases, over 30 years). Moreover, the firms in the former group have relatively young entrepreneurs (< 36 years old) who have limited working experience in the industry (less than six years); entrepreneurs/managers of firms in the latter group are older (over 54 years old) and with more extensive experience in the industry (over 15 years).

The variables concerning the perception of factors of success and constraints to entrepreneurial activity are also significant in explaining the first axis. Entrepreneurs/managers of the first group, consider morality, rationality and intelligence – variables that may be labelled as *stock* – among the personal qualities that assume greater importance for success; at the same time they hold that skills derived from technical, economic and market knowledge, whose acquisition – unlike stock variables – requires an active role on the part of the entrepreneur, have no effect upon success. Entrepreneurs in the second group appear to take the opposite stance on this issue, although the variables in question have a more limited weight in explaining axis variability.

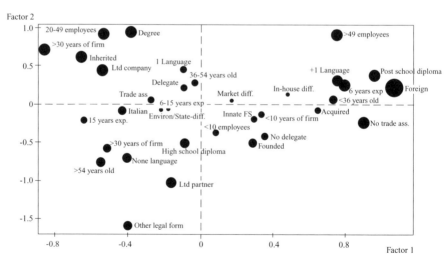

Figure 5.8 Factorial plan of active variables

The contrast between the two groups also emerges from an analysis of difficulties encountered by entrepreneurs in managing their respective transport business. For foreign entrepreneurs, market variables (absence of entry barriers, insufficiency of demand, difficulty in implementing forms of collaboration with competitors to achieve cost advantages) have considerable weight in this sense, while the difficulties measured by environmental variables (lack of services, lack of areas with facilities, environmental constraints, etc.) appear of little importance. By contrast, Italian entrepreneurs indicate an inverted scale of priorities, in which environmental variables assume a more significant position. A final element distinguishing the two groups of entrepreneurs concerns their involvement in Trade Associations which in the case of foreign entrepreneurs appears unimportant, while it is fairly common among Italian entrepreneurs.

The *second factorial axis* is significantly tied to information concerning the entrepreneur's human profile and to firm size. The positive semi-axis is explained by second or third generation entrepreneurs with an average age between 36 and 54, who have inherited the family business, with a high educational level (*Post-school diploma, degree*) and able to speak at least one foreign language. The firms in question were mainly established over 30 years ago, are slightly larger on average (> *15 employees*) and chiefly consist of limited companies.

The negative semi-axis is characterised by entrepreneurs who are no longer young (> *54 years old*), who only have a high-school diploma, and who founded their firm over ten years before. This group has fewer than 10 employees and consist of mainly privately-owned companies.

A further discriminating element between the two groups of entrepreneurs consists in the practice of delegating one or more business functions, or at least consulting staff in relation to particular choices. Analysis of the data shows that young entrepreneurs belonging to the former group leave greater autonomy to their staff, delegating administrative, financial or commercial management, or especially technical functions (production, information technology, quality), while those more advanced in years delegate much less.

The framework outlined above may be further enhanced by observation of the illustrative points which, though not participating directly in the construction of factors and thus not affecting their interpretation, contribute to completing the profile defined by observation of active categories. Only those with an absolute test-value greater than 2 (Table 5.8) were considered.

As may be deduced from Figure 5.9 – which reports the illustrative points projected on two axes – foreign firms managed by relatively young entrepreneurs who show greater pragmatism in business management (positive semi-axis of the first factor) only recently (< *6 years*) introduced ICT in the firm. They chiefly use standard software on a *main frame* computer. Of the main difficulties connected to the use and diffusion of such technology, these entrepreneurs assign first place to the risk of failing to ensure the confidential nature of data; next is the need to reorganise work, and the need to employ new professional figures. These entrepreneurs also believe that investments in information technology have contributed to improving their competitive position.

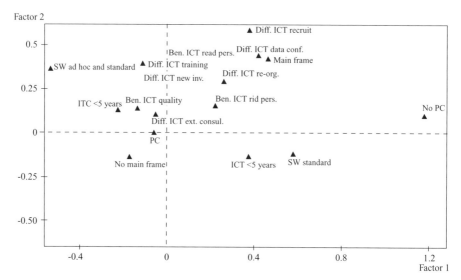

Figure 5.9 Factorial plan of illustrative variables

Italian entrepreneurs with considerable experience in the industry, characterising the negative semiaxis, show very poor ICT knowledge and the inability to perceive its importance in a transport market which is experiencing increasingly marked changes. These entrepreneurs introduced personal computers, with standard and bespoke software, into their firms at least five years ago, but they do not use this software for strategic processes able to significantly affect business efficiency. They also state that they have no fears regarding the confidentiality of their own data, perhaps due to the marginal functions performed by computers and the lack of interaction with the external environment.

Analysis of the arrangement of illustrative points on the second axis shows that the education level of entrepreneurs and the greater rootedness of the firm within the transport market affect the diffusion of information technology in the firm. Indeed, entrepreneurs with a higher educational level operating in more established firms on the transport market (positive semi-axis) widely use information technology; they generally have *main frame* computers that operate with bespoke software. The main difficulty encountered concerns staff training; however, other variables such as the need to reorganise work in the firm, high costs and data confidentiality, also play a non-marginal role in limiting investment in hardware and software. The more significant benefits include reductions in staffing costs and improvements in the customer service level, which have contributed to an overall enhancement of competitiveness.

In firms run by older entrepreneurs with less schooling (negative semi-axis), the level of ICT diffusion within the firm is low, if not totally absent. In particular, besides declaring a lack of computerisation, such entrepreneurs also show an incapacity to evaluate the difficulties and benefits of the use of ICT.

Cluster Analysis

It is widely known that cluster analysis, by reducing the space of individuals, makes it possible to find clusters which are as homogeneous as possible in themselves, yet as different as possible from other clusters. The clusters were defined by the co-ordinates of the first four factors of MCA. The results of the aggregation process allowed us to define 3 clusters.[4] To interpret these clusters, it is important to determine to what extent each category characterises a group. For this purpose we used a test value that has values close to zero when the category is not significant, and absolute increasing values as significance increases.[5]

As an empirical rule the chosen clusters are those with a test value greater than 2 in absolute terms.

The most significant categories of each class are reported in Table 5.9 in which, besides the test-value, the following information is reported:

♦ CLA/MOD: percentage of individuals that, of all those who indicated a certain response category, belong to the reference class;
♦ MOD/CLA: percentage of individuals of the sample who gave a certain category of response;
♦ GLOBAL: percentage of individuals of the sample that gave a certain category of response.

On the basis of such information the following entrepreneurial profiles may be defined.

Traditionals: (29%) these are the older constituents of the sample, of Italian nationality, who have managed their generally very small firms for a long time, and are found in market niches consisting of small segments in the logistics chain. Their existence is broadly linked to the particular structure of the Italian transport market, which is still very fragmented. The low education levels probably underlie the lack of a computer culture, which in effective terms translates into a lack of any ICT support for running their business. Indeed, they are unable to evaluate the difficulties or the benefits of using ICT, and thus represent those actors destined to be excluded from the transport chain as soon as the Italian market has become as mature as the most advanced markets worldwide.

Hopefuls: (45%) these form the largest class, the only one which can cope coherently with increasingly fierce and pervasive international competition on a domestic market which is ever more integrated with the international market. This group consists especially of very young, competent, well-educated Italian entrepreneurs who manage medium-size inherited firms. Compared with their predecessors, they stand for a management philosophy which is more open to environmental changes. However, this does not spill over into the implementation of advanced practices on all company levels; computerisation and the use of ICT are still at an initial phase and are thus unsuited to coping with the complexity of the market. The main company functions using ICT support concern only administration and finance. The possibility of growth is nevertheless tied to the ability of the entrepreneurs to overcome barriers to developing ICT, which in the future will no longer be a source of competitive advantage, but a prerequisite for operating in the transport market. In this sense, there is room for optimism, given that the main barriers do not appear to be cultural.

Innovators (26%): these are the intermediate class in numerical terms, consisting mainly of foreign entrepreneurs, also highly motivated, who show considerable knowledge of the constraints and opportunities afforded by the use of ICT. Though they do not have extensive operative experience, such entrepreneurs have recently become equipped with sophisticated information management systems that they nevertheless adopt with great caution, aware of the risks inherent in handling information. Rather than innovative, the entrepreneurs could be defined as "aware", given their ability to interpret business trends and, at the same time, arrange suitable operative systems to manage them efficiently.

Conclusions

In terms of the explanatory effectiveness of the model used, there emerges a significant discriminatory capacity in the analysis of ICT use in firms. The analysis undertaken showed that, in the presence of different characterisations of the entrepreneurial culture detected, the propensity to invest in hardware and software is motivated by stimuli that belong to the sphere of 'personal motivations' rather than the more rational sphere of the firm's economic convenience. Thus there seem to emerge models of entrepreneurial culture which are more linked to socio-entrepreneurial than economic-entrepreneurial variables (Ray, 1993). This result confirms the validity of the conceptual framework of the analysis of entrepreneurial culture through the entrepreneur's basic knowledge and technical and professional skills. However, there are broad margins for improving the conceptual framework, which may be achieved by introducing into the model further variables concerning the capacity to analyse *entrepreneurial behaviour* not considered in this work. This further aspect of entrepreneurial culture would contribute to increasing the model's discriminatory capacity.

With particular reference to the empirical evaluation model of the phenomenon in question

$$\Delta \text{ICT} = f(\text{CF, IF, FF})$$

statistical analysis shows that the firm-specific factors (FF) and the country-specific factors (CF) have greater influence than industrial factors (IF) in the introduction and use of ICT in the firms examined. Both in MCA and in cluster analysis, the contribution of variables of nationality and entrepreneurial culture is more discriminating on the factorial axes and on clusters than that of the variables which are representative of the various industries examined.

It thus significantly emerges that ICT diffusion in firms is tied in complex fashion to entrepreneurial profiles, which are highly subjective, making it difficult to identify and apply policies to support and promote ICT, which require objective points of references in order to be applied effectively and efficiently. Sectoral intervention policies at the European level thus appear inadvisable; there may be more valid forms of intervention on a national scale provided that homogeneous behavioural clusters are identified. But if the propensity to ICT is more *cross-firm* than *cross-industry*, considerable resources must still be invested in analysing methods to evaluate entrepreneurial phenomena in order to reach a modelling level which is sufficient to apply economic policies that can significantly affect the phenomenon.

Finally, considering the debate over the specific nature of the freight transport industry, these results are in line with the analysis already made by Vanroye and Blonk (1998) regarding the degree of ICT diffusion in the transport industry. In particular, they identify a series of endogenous and exogenous factors that limit ICT diffusion in the transport industry, which may be summarised as follows: a) traditional resistance to change on the part of transport operators; b) the small size of transport firms (especially in Europe) that do not have enough resources to finance investments in ICT and communication; c) the costs of using ICT; d) the use of appropriate standards by the most important actors in transport. However all these factors are strongly correlated with the determinants of entrepreneurial culture and thus not only tied to sectoral characteristics.

The use of modern ICT and communication instruments appears to be a necessary condition to emerge from the situation of marginality in which such firms are currently positioned. Only through the diffusion of various ICT and communication technologies, such as Electronic Data Interchange (EDI) and electronic trade (Internet), is it possible to achieve integration with other actors operating in the same transport chain and with customers. Indeed, for transport service suppliers, the use of the Internet has become an important tool for commercial, administrative and technical management as well as marketing. By the same token, the Internet has allowed shippers easier and more immediate access to information, thereby contributing to market transparency.

If appropriate and intense ICT use in the freight transport chain should, in the near future, become a significant discriminant of company competitiveness, we might expect great changes both to critical market factors and to the relative strength of the various actors present, insofar as the real factor of success in the short and medium-long run will be those *entrepreneurial profiles open to change and innovation*, unevenly distributed by country and industry.

Table 5.1 Factors of success or impediments to the growth of entrepreneurial firms

Factors of success

	Innate personal qualities		Acquired personal qualities		External factors of success	
	Important	Less important	Important	Less important	Important	Less important
Italian	48.02	51.98	58.42	41.58	12.87	87.13
Foreign	56.52	43.48	50.00	50.00	28.26	71.74

Operative difficulties

	Market variables		In house variables		Environmental variables	
	Important	Less important	Important	Less important	Important	Less important
Italian	58.42	41.58	6.93	93.07	17.82	82.18
Foreign	74.47	25.53	6.38	93.62	2.13	97.87

Difficulties of introducing IT

	Staff training		Resources for Investments		Data confidentiality	
	Important	Less important	Important	Less important	Important	Less important
Italian	43.43	56.57	37.76	62.24	18.75	81.25
Foreign	50.00	50.00	42.55	57.45	52.17	47.83

Benefits of introducing IT

	Employees reduction		Service level enhancement		Competition improvement	
	Important	Less important	Important	Less important	Important	Less important
Italian	81.25	18.75	93.81	6.19	48.42	51.58
Foreign	72.34	27.66	78.72	21.28	74.47	25.53

Table 5.2 Distribution of interviewees by age and degree of IT diffusion in the firm

IT diffusion								
	Absent		Limited		High		Total	
	N.	%	N.	%	N.	%	N.	%
< 35	3	20.00	7	21.88	25	26.04	35	24.48
35 – 54	11	73.33	19	59.37	48	50.00	78	54.55
> 54	1	6.67	6	18.75	23	23.96	30	20.98
Total	15	10.49	32	22.38	96	67.13	143	100.00

Table 5.3 Active variables

Variables	1st category	2nd category	3rd category	4th category
Nationality	Italian	Foreign		
Entrepreneurial experience	– 6 years	6 – 15 years	+ 15 years	
Type of ownership	Inherited	Founded	Acquired	
Entrepreneur's age	<36	36-54	>54	
Educational qualification	High school diploma	Post-school diploma	Degree	
Foreign languages known	None	One	More than one	
Trade Association membership	No	Yes		
Innate factor of success	Yes	No		
Acquired factor of success	Yes	No		
External factor of success	Yes	No		
Delegates responsibility	No	Yes		
Market operative difficulties	Yes	No		
In-house operative difficulties	Yes	No		
Environmental/State operative difficulties	Yes	No		
Legal form	Limited partnership	Limited company	Other	
Firm's age	< 10 years	10 – 30 years	> 30 years	
Number of employees	< 10	10 – 19	20 - 49	> 49

Table 5.4 Illustrative variables

Variables	1st category	2nd category	3rd category
N° of years of ICT in the firm.	< 5	> 5	
Availability of ICT tools in the firm	None	Low	High
Specific ICT tools available in the firm			
– Telematic Systems	No	Yes	
– PC	No	Yes	
– Main frame	No	Yes	
– Server	No	Yes	
– Web site	No	Yes	
– Others facilities	No	Yes	
Software used (Sw)	Ad hoc	Standard	Ad hoc and standard
Constraints to introduction of ICT			
– Lack of information	Less important	Important	
– Lack of specialist personnel	Less important	Important	
– High costs	Less important	Important	
– Re-organisation of labour in the firm	Less important	Important	
– Data confidentiality	Less important	Important	
Application of ICT			
– ICT for Technical function	No	Yes	
– ICT for Administrative function	No	Yes	
– ICT for Financial function	No	Yes	
– ICT for Commercial function	No	Yes	
– ICT for Others	No	Yes	
Difficulties encountered in ICT introduction			
– Use of external consultants	Less important	Important	
– Training of personnel	Less important	Important	
– Recruitment of qualified personnel	Less important	Important	
– Re-organisation of labour in the firm	Less important	Important	
– New investments	Less important	Important	
– Data confidentiality	Less important	Important	
Benefits from ICT introduction			
– Increase in productivity	Less important	Important	
– Improvement in service quality	Less important	Important	
– Staff reduction	Less important	Important	
– Improvement in competitiveness	Less important	Important	

Table 5.5 Diagram of the percentages of variability explained by Eigenvalues

	Eigen values	explained variance %	Cumulative Variance %	
1	0.1572	10.41	10.41	***
2	0.1338	8.86	19.27	**
3	0.1054	6.98	26.25	***
4	0.0945	6.26	32.51	**************************************
5	0.0861	5.70	38.21	*************************************
6	0.0825	5.46	43.68	**********************************
7	0.0749	4.96	48.64	*********************************
8	0.0697	4.61	53.25	********************************
9	0.0627	4.15	57.40	******************************
10	0.0589	3.83	61.24	*****************************
11	0.0564	3.73	64.97	****************************
12	0.0531	3.52	68.49	***************************
13	0.0501	3.32	71.81	**************************
14	0.0498	3.30	75.11	*************************
15	0.0445	2.95	78.06	**********************
16	0.0419	2.77	80.83	*********************
17	0.0374	2.48	83.31	*******************
18	0.0351	2.33	85.64	******************
19	0.0317	2.10	87.73	*****************
20	0.0292	1.94	89.67	****************
21	0.0275	1.82	91.49	***************
22	0.0249	1.65	93.14	*************
23	0.0216	1.43	94.57	************
24	0.0200	1.33	95.90	***********
25	0.0177	1.17	97.07	**********
26	0.0140	0.92	97.99	*********
27	0.0130	0.86	98.86	********
28	0.0118	0.78	99.64	********
29	0.0037	0.24	99.88	**
30	0.0016	0.10	99.98	*
31	0.0002	0.02	100.00	*

Table 5.6 Corrected Eigenvalues

	Eigenvalues	explained variance %	Cumulative Variance %
1	0.1572	26.08	26.08
2	0.1338	18.90	44.98
3	0.1054	11.73	56.71
4	0.0945	9.43	66.13
5	0.0861	7.82	73.96
6	0.0825	7.18	81.14
7	0.0749	5.92	87.06
8	0.0697	5.13	92.19
9	0.0627	4.15	96.34
10	0.0589	3.66	100.0

Table 5.7 Absolute contributions and value test of active variables

Variables	Coordinates		Contributions		Test values	
Categories	1	2	1	2	1	2
NATIONALITY						
• Italian	-0.43	-0.08	4.6	0.2	-7.64	-1.49
• Foreign	1.11	0.22	12.6	0.6	9.15	1.84
Cumulative contribution =			17.2	0.8		
ENTREPRENURIAL EXPERIENCE						
• - 6 years exp	0.86	0.24	7.9	0.7	6.92	1.89
• 6 - 15 years exp	-0.18	-0.05	0.5	0.1	-1.93	-0.58
• + 15 years exp.	-0.64	-0.21	3.6	0.4	-4.43	-1.43
Cumulative contribution =			12.0	1.2		
TYPE OF OWNERSHIP						
• Inherited	-0.65	0.62	5.2	5.5	-5.66	5.35
• Founded	0.29	-0.51	1.4	5.1	3.38	-5.94
• Acquired	0.65	-0.08	1.3	0.0	2.45	-0.29
Cumulative contribution =			7.9	10.6		
ENTREPRENEUR'S AGE						
• <36 years old	0.73	0.07	4.6	0.0	5.05	0.45
• 36-54 years old	-0.03	0.27	0.0	1.6	-0.38	3.45
• > 54 years old	-0.55	-0.77	2.2	5.1	-3.43	-4.79
Cumulative contribution =			6.8	6.7		

EDUCATIONAL QUALIFICATION

• High school diploma	-0.08	-0.51	0.1	6.0	-1,16	-7.05
• Post-school diploma	0.96	0.39	5.9	1.1	5.63	2.28
• Degree	-0.42	0.95	1.5	9.1	-2.84	6.44
Cumulative contribution	=	7.5	16.3			

FOREIGN LANGUAGES KNOWN

• None language	-0.40	-0.70	1.8	6.3	-3.28	-5.68
• 1 language	-0.09	0.46	0.1	3.1	-0.81	4.15
• + 1 language	0.82	0.29	5.9	0.9	5.84	2.08
Cumulative contribution	=	7.8	10.3			

TRADE ASSOCIATION MEMBERSHIP

• No_Trade Ass.	1.05	-0.16	8.5	0.2	6.84	-1.02
• Trade Ass.	-0.27	0.05	2.0	0.1	-6.04	1.21
Cumulative contribution	=	10.5	0.3			

INNATE FACTOR OF SUCCESS

• Innate FS	0.29	-0.18	1.7	0.7	3.93	-2.43
• No_innate FS	-0.28	0.27	1.2	1.3	-3.06	2.90
Cumulative contribution	=	2.9	2.1			

ACQUIRED FACTOR OF SUCCESS

• No_acquired FS	-0.14	0.09	0.4	0.2	2.73	-0.78
• Acquired FS	0.25	-0.07	1.0	0.1	-1.87	1.27
Cumulative contribution	=	1.4	0.3			

EXTERNAL FACTOR OF SUCCESS

• No_external FS	0.28	0.17	0.5	0.2	-0.45	-0.31
• External FS	-0.02	-0.01	0.0	0.0	1.58	0.96
Cumulative contribution	=	0.5	0.2			

DELEGATES RESPONSIBILITY

• No_delegate	0.35	-0.43	1.3	2.2	2.79	-3.37
• Delegate	-0.09	0.21	0.2	1.2	-1.64	3.75
Cumulative contribution	=	1.5	3.4			

MARKET OPERATIVE DIFFICULTIES

• Market diff.	0.18	0.06	0.7	0.1	2.80	0.96
• No_ market diff.	-0.21	-0.08	0.6	0.1	-1.92	-0.72
Cumulative contribution	=	1.2	0.2			

IN-HOUSE OPERATIVE DIFFICULTIES

• In-house diff.	0.48	0.13	0.5	0.0	1.57	0.41
• No_In-house diff.	0.00	0.00	0.0	0.0	0.12	0.04
Cumulative contribution	=	0.5	0.0			

ENVIRONMENTAL/STATE OPERATIVE DIFFICULTIES

• Environm/State diff.	-0.28	-1.17	0.4	7.3	-2.32	-0.77
• No_Environm/ State diff.	0.08	0.18	0.2	1.2	3.16	1.00
Cumulative contribution =			0.6	8.6		

LEGAL FORM

• Ltd. partnership	-0.16	-1.04	0.2	8.4	-0.93	-5.94
• Ltd company	-0.54	0.46	4.6	3.8	-5.71	4.83
• Other legal form.	-0.40	-1.63	0.3	5.3	-1.08	-4.40
Cumulative contribution =			5.0	17.6		

FIRM'S AGE

• <10 years of firm	0.34	-0.15	1.1	0.2	2.44	-1.06
• 10-30 years of firm	-0.51	-0.59	2.7	4.2	-3.90	-4.47
• > 30 years of firm	-0.88	0.70	4.5	3.3	-4,69	3.72
Cumulative contribution =			8.3	7.7		

NUMBER OF EMPLOYEES

• < 10 employees	0.08	-0.37	0.1	3.2	1.12	-5.00
• 10-19 employees	-0.11	-0.02	0.1	0.0	-0.59	
• 20-49 employees	-0.59	0.93	1.7	5.0	-2.90	4.56
• >49 employees	0.75	0.97	2.2	4.5	3.38	4.40
Cumulative contribution =			4.2	12.7		

Table 5.8 Test values of coordinates of illustrative points on the first and second axis

VARIABLES	CATEGORIES	VALORE TEST	
		1	2
N° of years of ICT in the firm	ICT >5 years	-2.82	
	ICT <5 years	3.91	
Specific ICT tools available in the firm			
– PC	PC	-2.52	
	No_PC	3.64	
– Main frame	No_main frame	-2.13	-2.68
	Main frame	2.94	2.73
Software used (Sw)	Sw ad hoc and standard	-3.83	2.59
	Sw standard	5.72	
Application of ICT			
– Financial function	No_ICT finan. func.	-3.42	-3.12
	ICT finan func.	2.66	3.16
– Others	No_ICT.other func.	-5.58	
Difficulties encountered in ICT introduction			
– Use of external consultants	Diff. ICT Ext onsul. No_imp.	1.91	
– Training of personnel	Diff. ICT training No_imp	2.03	-4.25
	Diff. ICT training		4.33
– Recruitment of qualified personnel	Diff. ICT recruitm	2.36	3.66
	Diff. ICT Recruitm No_imp.		-3.75
– Re-organisation of labour in the firm	Diff. ICT re-organis.	2.85	3.25
	Diff. ICT re-organis. No_imp		-3.61
– New investments	Diff. ICT new inv. No_imp.		-2.71
	Diff. ICT new inv.		2.97
– Data confidentiality	Diff. ICT data conf. No_imp	-2.16	-3.31
	Diff. ICT data conf.	3.19	3.42
Benefits derived from ICT introduction			
– Improvement in service quality	Ben. ICT > qualità		2.81
– Staff reduction	Ben._ ICT rid.person. No_imp		-2.13
	Ben._ ICT rid.person.		3.29
– Improvement in competitiveness	Imp_ben.ICT competit.	2.93	2.11
	Ben.ICT competit. No_Imp	-1.59	-1.12

Table 5.9 Clusters

VARIABLES	CATEGORIES	GLOBAL	MOD/ CLA	CLA/ MOD	V.TEST
First Cluster: 29.05% of cases					
Firm's age	10-30 years of firm	28.38	65.12	66.67	6.00
Legal form	Ltd. Partnership	18.24	46.51	74.07	5.24
Educational qualification	High school diploma	56.76	88.37	45.24	5.03
Foreign languages known	No language	31.08	60.47	56.52	4.65
Type of ownership	Founded	47.97	76.74	46.48	4.37
Entrepreneur's age	>54	20.95	44.19	61.29	4.07
ICT for financial function	No_ICT finan. func.	47.97	74.42	45.07	3.99
Nationality	Italian	68.24	90.70	38.61	3.79
Legal form	Other legal form	4.73	16.28	100.0	3.67
Recruitment of qualified personnel	Diff. ICT recruit. No_imp.	76.35	95.35	36.28	3.56
Number of employees	< 10 employees	54.73	76.74	40.74	3.32
Training of personnel	Diff. ICT traini. No_imp	53.38	72.09	39.24	2.77
Main frame	No_main frame	75.00	90.70	35.14	2.75
Re-organisation of labour in the firm	Diff. ITC re-organis. No_imp	51.35	69.77	39.47	2.71
Data confidentiality	Diff. ICT data conf. No_imp	67.57	83.72	36.00	2.57
Improv. of competitive edge	Ben. ICT compet No_Imp	41.22	58.14	40.98	2.48
Second Cluster: 45.27% of cases					
Legal form	Ltd. Company	43.24	77.61	81.25	7.76
Educational qualification	Degree	23.65	47.76	91.43	6.35
Type of ownership	Inherited	33.78	59.70	80.00	6.01
Nationality	Italian	68.24	92.54	61.39	5.89
Software used (Sw)	Sw ad hoc and standard	25.68	43.28	76.32	4.32
Firm's age	>30 years	16.22	29.85	83.33	3.95
Number of employees	20-49 employees	14.19	25.37	80.95	3.36
ICT for Administrative func.	ICT adm. func	80.41	92.54	52.10	3.28
Delegates responsibility	Delegate	68.92	82.09	53.92	3.01
External factor of success	No_external FS	81.76	92.54	51.24	2.96
Foreign languages known	1 language	35.81	47.76	60.38	2.59
Acquired factor of success	Acquired FS	55.41	67.16	54.88	2.46

Third Cluster: 25.68% of cases

Nationality	Foreign	31.76	100.00	80.85	10.71
Software used (Sw)	Sw standard	39.86	78.95	50.85	5.54
Educational qualification	Post-high school dipl	18.92	44.74	60.71	4.23
Data confidentiality difficulties	Imp._data conf. Diff.	28.38	55.26	50.00	3.93
Foreign languages known	+1 language	25.68	50.00	50.00	3.64
Main frame	Main frame	21.62	44.74	53.13	3.62
Trade Association membership	No_Trade Ass.	22.30	44.74	51.52	3.48
Difficulties in re-organing labour	Diff. ICT re-organis.	44.59	68.42	39.39	3.25
Number of employees	>49 employees	12.16	28.95	61.11	3.18
Difficulties in recruiting qualified personnel	Imp_recruitm diff.	20.95	39.47	48.39	2.92
Improv. of competi-tiveness from ICT	Ben ICT competit.	54.73	73.68	34.57	2.57
N° of years of ICT in the firm	ICT <5 years	42.57	60.53	36.51	2.40
Entreprenurial experience	- 6 years esp	30.41	47.37	40.00	2.39
PC	No PC	6.08	15.79	66.67	2.36

Notes

1   For an in-depth analysis of issues related to the various ways of applying methods of multivariate analysis see Del Vecchio, 1992.
2   In our case $1/17=0.0588$, hence only the first 10 eigenvalues are considered.
3   The table of absolute contributions provides, for each active category and for each axis, the percentage of axis variability explained by the point.
4   The hierarchical classification method used is agglomerative, i.e. it starts from n distinct firms considered as n groups on their own and, at each analytical step, aggregates the two units or two classes so that the new class satisfies a set grouping criterion. In classifying the various firms we used Ward's criterion as a grouping criterion which, at each analytical step, aggregates the pair of observations that minimises the variance of the new clusters obtained.
5   This measurement is obtained by comparing, for each response, the percentage frequencies observed in the same group with the total percentage frequencies: the more the values differ, the more that group is characterised by the response type.

References

Argyris, C. and Schon, D.A. (1978), *Organizational Learning: a Theory of Action Perspective*, Reading, Massachusetts, Addison-Wesley Publishing.

Bull, I. and Willard, G.E. (1993), 'A Perspective on Theory Building in Entrepreneurship', *Journal of Business Venturing*, Vol. 8 no. 3, pp. 183-195.

Bygrave, W.D. (1993), 'Theory Building in the Entrepreneurship Paradigm', *Journal of Business Venturing*, Vol. 8 no. 3, pp. 255-280.

Del Vecchio, F. (1992), *Analisi statistica di dati multidimensionali*, Cacucci Editore, Bari.

Evangelista P., Morvillo, A. (1998), 'The role of training in developing entrepreneurship: the case of shipping in Italy', *Maritime Policy & Management*, Vol. 25 no.1, pp. 81-96.

Garvin, D.A. (1993), 'Building a Learning Organization', *Harvard Business Review*, Vol.71 no. 4, pp. 78-91.

Hendry, J. and Hope, V. (1994), 'Cultural Change and Competitive Performance', *European Management Journal*, Vol. 12 no. 4, pp. 401-406.

Hofstede, G. (1994), 'The Business of International Business is Culture', *International Business Review*, Vol. 3 no. 1, pp. 1-30.

Huber, G.P. (1991), 'Organisational Learning, The Contributing Processes and the Literature', *Organisation Science*, Vol. 2 no.1, pp. 88-115.

Kotter, J.P. and Heskett, J.L. (1992), *Corporate Culture and Performances*, New York, Free Press.

McDougall, P.P. (1989), 'International Versus Domestic Entrepreneurship: New Venture Strategic Behaviour and Industry Structure', *Journal of Business Venturing*, Vol. 4 no. 6, pp. 387-400.

McGrath, R.G., MacMillan, I.C., and Scheinberg, S. (1992), 'Elitists, Risk-Takers, and Rugged Individualists? An Exploratory Analysis of Cultural Differences Between Entrepreneurs and Non-Entrepreneurs', *Journal of Business Venturing*, Vol. 7 no. 2, pp. 115-135.

Minguzzi, A., Passaro, R. (1997), 'Apprentissage et culture d'entreprise dans les PME: une analyse explorative intersectorielle', *Revue Internationale PME*, Vol. 10 no. 2.

Minguzzi, A., Passaro, R. (2000), 'The relations system between the economic environment and the entrepreneurial culture in small firms', *Journal of Business Venturing*, Vol. 16 no. 2, pp. 181-207.

Nonaka, I., Takeuchi, H. (1997), *The knowledge-creating company. Creare le dinamiche dell'innovazione*. Milan, Guerini. Eds. Frigelli U, Inumaru K.

Ray, D. (1993), 'Open and Bounded Entrepreneurship', *Journal of Small Business Entrepreneurship*, Vol. 9 no. 3, pp. 89-100.

Sackmann, S.A. (1991), *Cultural Knowledge in Organizations*, London, Sage Publications.

Schein, E.H. (1984), 'Cultura organizzativa e processi di cambiamento aziendali', *Sviluppo & Organizzazione*, no. 84, pp. 115-129.

Schein, E.H. (1992), *Organizational Culture and Leadership*, San Francisco, Jossey-Bass Publishers.

Schumpeter, J.A. (1934), *The Theory of Economic Development*, Cambridge, Harvard University Press.

Slevin, D.P. and Covin, J.G. (1990), 'Juggling Entrepreneurial Style and Organizational Structure – How to Get your Act Together', *Sloan Management Review*, 32.

Smith, P.B. and Peterson, M.F. (1988), *Leadership, Organizations and Culture*, London, Sage Publications.

Vanroye, K. & Blonk, W.A.G. (1998), 'The creation of an information highway for intermodal transport', *Maritime Policy & Management*, 25 (3):263-268.

PART II

PLANNING AND EXECUTION OF A TRAINING PROJECT IN THE INDUSTRY: METHODOLOGY, RESULTS AND IMPLICATIONS

Chapter 6

Flexibility and Personalisation of Training Paths in the FIT Project

Gennaro Ferrara

Objective of the FIT Project

As a result of the dynamics within the logistics and freight transport industry, highlighted in the first part of the book, there is an urgent need for training and vocational training at operational and managerial levels. Indeed, professional retraining of human resources – which stimulates the capability of reacting to the industry's exogenous and endogenous demands – is, at the micro level, a source of competitive advantage and, at the macro level, an effective tool in the implementation of employment-oriented policies.

In order satisfy the human resource needs to adjust to industrial changes (a need also felt in many other sectors of the economic activity), the European Union has promoted some initiatives, including the ADAPT Program. In the period 1995-1999 this Program funded approximately 4000 projects, all of them aimed at preserving the present employment level and creating new job opportunities.[1]

Within the framework of this Program, the FIT Project was the result of joint action between the academic, research and entrepreneurial fields to boost transport and logistics activities in the Region of Campania.

The aim of the project was to create proper conditions for job flexibility, meant as the capability of the labour force to perform different functions both within the same firm and in other firms of the logistics *filière*, in response to current evolutionary dynamics.

The project is innovative in that the training provision does not include a unique training path but a set of paths, the number of which is defined by the choices made by the users following appropriate vocational guidance.

It is worth stressing the experimental nature of the project whose implementation required a great deal of effort owing to its innovative nature compared to other training activities performed in Campania, and also to the high number of participants (10% of those employed in the target industry).

The Original Project

The original project included development and implementation of 20 training and vocational re-training courses, differentiated according to the various segments of the transport *filière*. Each course consisted of 20 operators.

The analysis of the training needs and the resulting identification of the professional profiles on which training and training paths (meant as curricula) had to be focused, were made with the support of the Trade Associations involved in the Project as partners.[2] Some courses addressed specific professional figures in the transport *filière (shipping agents, clearing agents, freight forwarders, terminal operators, hauliers, etc.)*, while other courses included subjects such as *finance, marketing* and *quality*, which could be of interest to each of the target professional figures. Each course had a duration of 210 hours, for a total amount of 84,000 hours/trained student (20 students x 20 courses x 210 hours per course).

Each course was sub-divided into the following three modules:

♦ 'Basic' module (45 hours), aimed at providing the basic skills to be performed in the sector;
♦ 'Supports and Tools' module (65 hours), aimed at providing the basic elements of the English language (also technical language) and computer science. These subjects which were supposed to be included in the basic module have, instead, been considered as separate modules as a result of the importance attached to them by entrepreneurs when analysis of the training needs was conducted;
♦ 'Specialisation module' (100 hours), aimed at increasing the specific technical-professional competence of each operator.

Thanks to uninterrupted and widespread promotion, begun prior to the final approval of the Project, four courses had already been initiated at the beginning of June1998:

♦ Sea freight operators
♦ Freight forwarders
♦ Shipping agents
♦ Hauliers.

The constant monitoring performed by tutors, however, underscored the difficulty of students to comply with the minimum attendance requirements (number of days stipulated by the Social Fund) and with the predefined training objectives. For this reason the above courses were suspended.

Subsequently, attention was focused chiefly on two crucial aspects for the success of the training initiative:

♦ To what extent had the project idea been developed in line with the 'culture' of course participants and of the entrepreneurial world?
♦ Did the curricula have the 'right balance' between the need to provide a set of competencies (as suggested by the analysis of the training needs) and the need of the individual participants to follow a path which, starting from the competencies already acquired, was consistent with their requirements, skills and potentials?

It was crucial to understand these points in order to pursue job flexibility, which was the aim and the underlying philosophy of the project. The first aspect was investigated by means of a thorough analysis of the qualitative features of middle and top management in the Region of Campania, conducted in an empirical survey, involving all categories in the transport *filière*. In particular, given the interest shown by the transnational partners of the project in entrepreneurial culture and in its relationship to dissemination of Innovation Technology in the industry, the survey became a supra-national survey which gave rise to a *cross-country analysis*, the results of which are illustrated in Chapter 5.

The outcomes relating exclusively to Campania highlighted the presence of a prevailing culture characterised by artisan-like business management, totally unsuited to the industry's specificity and complexity. The interviews also showed how local operators focused principally on the technical aspects of training, which is mainly characterised by a *learning by doing* approach.

Within this framework 'structured training', though officially viewed as extremely important, was not actually perceived as a leverage for development. This cultural approach to training, typical of small firms, emerged very clearly from the interviews with entrepreneurs. In actual facts, while willing to co-operate in developing curricula and identifying the most qualified and suitable teachers, they explicitly demanded that courses be held outside of working hours.

For this reason courses were held two or three days a week and each class lasted no more than 2 hours. Based on this time tabling, each course lasted from 8 to 13 months, with the resulting difficulty of keeping high both motivation and participation of the trainees.

With reference to the analysis of the impact the course structure had on job flexibility, some doubts were raised on the capability of the training provision to meet the variability of training needs. This problem could have been solved by arranging classes with a variable number of students according to the interest shown by each of them in the specific modules. However, this solution conflicted with bureaucratic and administrative requirements, implying a set of constraints that were necessary at any rate to monitor the training activities.

Adjusting the Training Activity to the Students' Needs

In the revised as in the original project, training paths were defined on the basis of the needs of the individual operators in the transport filière. However, greater attention was placed on the need to adopt a more flexible structure and module-based training.

The activity of each professional profile (clearing agent, freight forwarder, shipping agent, terminal operator, road haulier, etc.) may be broken down into *Processes*, meant as a sequence of flows of activities which are directly interconnected and aimed at producing a specific result. Within each Process precise *Areas of Activity* are defined, each of them meant as the whole set of specific, homogeneous and integrated activities aimed at producing a result. In pursuing this approach, a precise Area of Activity can be found in more than one Process, and a specific Process may involve various operators (see Chapter 7).

Competencies required in each Area of Activity were then included in a specific didactic module (see Appendix 1 'Courses developed in the FIT project').

Based upon this methodological approach, each of the potential candidates for the training courses could develop his/her own training path by combining different modules with the following variables: a) competencies already possessed; b) competencies which he/she should acquire based upon the standard profile; c) competencies that he/she would like to acquire.

In line with this approach, the *guidance/assessment* objective was to:

♦ identify the competencies already held;
♦ identify and select a personalised training path through modules or training units.

Two general objectives were achieved through the FIT project:

♦ the start of many separate training paths aimed at adjusting individual competencies to the threshold competencies of each professional profile, which could later be continued once the project came to an end;
♦ the organisation of training courses aimed at developing new competencies, thereby enabling those already in place to be optimised and new competencies to be brought out.

The original project provided for a total amount of 84,000 hours of training. As a result of the changes introduced, the total number of hours was subdivided differently and allocated to the various training courses within the project. These changes may be summarised as follows:

♦ Some training modules with a 35-hour duration were developed, each of which addressed to 20 students and focused on a topic of interest dealt with in a thorough manner.
♦ Each student defined his/her training path by selecting a combination of sequential training modules. (see Figure 6.1).

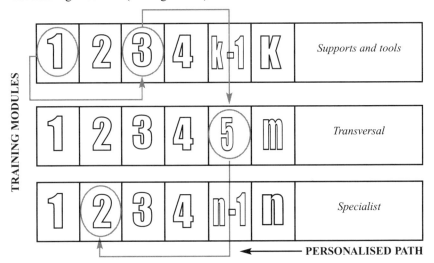

Figure 6.1 Flexible training paths

♦ The duration of the training path in terms of n° of modules, and then of total number of hours, was not defined a priori for all students (see Figure 6.2). Duration was decided on the basis of a set of factors which included working conditions in the specific transport *filière*, level of competence before starting the course and the targeted professional level.

♦ The total amount of *training hours/trained student*, corresponding to the summation of the training hours of all participants, was equal to the amount provided for in the original project.

♦ Because of reporting and auditing reasons, each module was *independent* of the other modules from the bureaucratic-administrative standpoint and from this perspective it was considered as a course. For each course a selection of the participants was made, a separate register to record attendance kept and a specific report written.

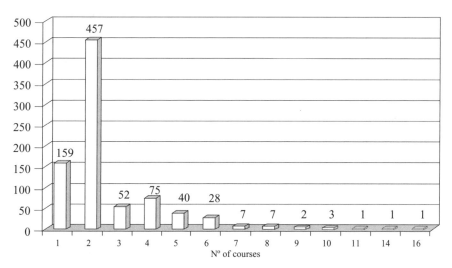

Figure 6.2 Total number of courses attended per number of trainees

♦ The composition of each class (20 trainees) was often heterogeneous, i.e. the course participants did not only include those interested in the specific competencies required for a given profile in the transport *filière*. This was particularly true for those competencies related to Areas of Activity common to more Processes, i.e. related to Processes which can be found in different professional profiles.

In synthesis, the composition of the training path for an individual participant (including modules x, y and z, rather than modules x, r, s) was based upon his/her inclinations and motivations. In personalising the training path, it was possible for the participants to optimise their time for training purposes, taking into account the constraints of their working terms and conditions.

Insofar as the number of editions for each planned course is concerned, the results of the FIT project are found below, in Figures 6.3 and 6.4.

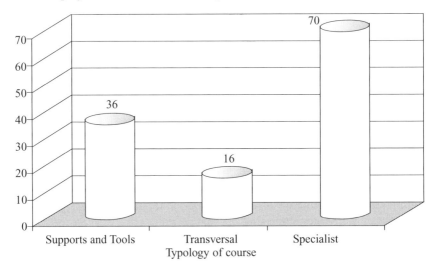

Figure 6.3 Number of course editions

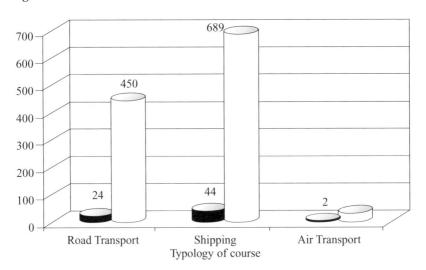

Figure 6.4 Number of course editions and total number of participants per group of specialist courses

Appendix 1 Courses developed in the FIT project

Group 1: SUPPORTS AND TOOLS

For the operators who need to develop the operative skills to work in an efficient way.
1. English for Beginners
2. Intermediate English
3. Advanced English
4. Introduction to computing
5. Word and Excel
6. Relational databases-Access
7. Internet
8. Internet and Transport
9. Geographic Information Systems
10. Databases and principles of descriptive statistics
11. Exploratory analysis of multi-dimensional data
12. Time Series Analysis and forecasting methods
13. Explanatory analysis of multi-dimensional data

Group 2: TRANSVERSAL

For managers and decision-makers to update their knowledge of current trends in the area of transport and logistics.
1. Transport documents
2. General accounting
3. IVA (Value Added Tax): General regime and intra-EU regime
4. Transport insurance
5. The Euro and transport firms
6. Customer management and loyalty schemes
7. Transport marketing
8. Transport and EU legislation
9. Business Plan
10. International Taxation
11. Customs legislation and procedures
12. Strategic finance
13. Human resource management
14. Logistics and transport firms
15. Quality and logistics

Group 3: SPECIALIST

Technical-normative issues related to the specific transport segment: road transport, shipping and air transport.

ROAD TRANSPORT

1. Road transport legislation
2. Access to the road haulage market
3. Financial and commercial management of road haulage firms
4. Technical aspects of road transport
5. Road safety and international transport
6. Road transport of hazardous freight (Basic)
7. Road transport of hazardous freight (Advanced)
8. Law and rules in road transport

SHIPPING

1. Introduction to maritime English
2. Maritime English (Basic)
3. Maritime English (Advanced)
4. SMS-Safety Management Systems (Basic)
5. SMS-Safety Management (Advanced)
6. Naval computing
7. Naval automation
8. Advanced naval computing-AMOS
9. First aid
10. Vessel regulations and administration
11. International navigation law
12. Transport of hazardous goods
13. GMDSS (Basic)
14. GMDSS (Advanced)
15. GMDSS (Application)

AIR TRANSPORT

1. Transport of hazardous goods
2. Legislation and fees (Basic)
3. Legislation, fees and transport of hazardous goods (Advanced)

Notes

1   From 1995 to 1999, ADAPT focused primarily on the following themes:
    * new forms for work organisations
    * the implications of flexibility
    * SMEs and anticipation
    * cooperation and networking
    * SMEs and continuing training.

2   Although the project partners worked closely with one another, they each had a specific role to cover. The Istituto Universitario Navale (IUN – Naval University Institute) – presently named Università degli Studi di Napoli Parthenope (University of Studies Parthenope, Naples) – as the Promoter of the project, was accountable to the Ministry of Labour for the whole project; in addition to providing logistics support for course management, IUN provided some guidelines in the implementation and monitoring stages. The other partners were: Autorità Portuale di Napoli (AP-Port Authority of Naples); Associazione Campana Corrieri Spedizionieri e Autotrasportatori (ACCSEA – Association of Freight Forwarders, Couriers and Hauliers of the Region Campania); Associazione Nazionale degli Spedizionieri Doganali (Association of Clearing Agents); Collegio dei Capitani di Lungo Corso di Napoli (Board of Merchant Captains); Federazione Autotrasportatori Italiani (FAI – Federation of Italian Hauliers); Associazione Culturale per il Mare (ACMA – Marine Cultural Association); Hermes Srl (an IT provider in maritime transport).

Chapter 7

The Analysis of Training Needs: Methods and Techniques

Valentina Carbone

Introduction

Designing a professional training course entails defining all the aspects of the training situation (training needs, teaching objectives, learning conditions, teaching methods, organisational aspects) and harmonising them within an integrated, coherent system (Fontana, 1989).

Design is thus a construct which derives from an intentional, rational and purposeful process. It is also a structured set of targeted activities which are conditional upon the existence of a certain 'context' of actions, resources and constraints (Lipari, 1987). From this definition there clearly emerges the meta-disciplinary nature of design: it is both a global and systemic process and, at the same time, a logical process in methodological terms. Such a process may be divided into two phases, the 'informative system' and 'operative system'. Training Needs Analysis (TNA) feeds the informative system, which also includes the phase of results evaluation; whereas the operative system includes the steps of module planning and training realisation (Quaglino, 1985).

In its broadest meaning, TNA, in training and employment policies, surveys and analyses training and professional needs in a specific context: a geographical area or an industry. TNA acts as a link between the training system and productive system; it ensures a constant contribution to reviewing training provision at the national level (ISFOL, 1996).

Before presenting the current national policies concerning training needs anticipation in Europe and describing the different analytical methods, it should be emphasised that the phrase 'training needs analysis' can be used with different meanings: we can talk of simple observation or interpretation and/or anticipation of training needs. When we refer to 'observation' we support the idea of 'hard', 'objective' needs, which already exist, independently of the social actors' awareness. In this case, there only has to be an awareness of the training needs. By contrast, 'interpretation' and even more 'anticipation', support the idea of needs to analyse, interpret, and 'filter' through some kind of lens. Needs are established by an analyst (a single person, a team, an organisation) who produces them as the result of a survey, filtration and interpretation (Bresciani. *et al*, 1992).

It is widely argued, nowadays, that training is not a dependent variable, but that it interacts with the labour market and with the development of local productive systems. This means that training has to anticipate, not follow needs (OBNF, 2000).

After placing the phenomenon within its conceptual framework, the following section will present the development of policies to anticipate training needs in European countries. The next stage will consist in interpreting needs analysis as a planning tool to aid those involved in training and it is with reference to this definition that the most widely used techniques for TNA are addressed, examining the factors that determine the choice of the proper technique. Subsequently, attention will be focused on the approach adopted in the management of the training project in the domain of transport and logistics in southern Italy: FIT 'Integrated Transnational Training', developed within the ADAPT II Phase Framework. Finally, TNA results within the project will be presented and analysed.

Training Needs Analysis in European Union Member States

Most European countries possess structures, procedures and activities which aim to anticipate the training needs of production systems as a result of technological and organisational changes. Major experience gained in several EU countries may be a useful reference point in a phase in which Italy is attempting to develop from a situation with a large number of models and tools in various areas and sectors to the definition of a single general model at national level.

The various contexts for training needs in each EU country were analysed according to three criteria: institutional context, the role of the government and analytical tools used. By evaluating the degree of institutional involvement and the level of sophistication of analytical tools adopted, the criteria are used to effectively represent the evolution of training needs analysis in the various countries. Indeed, where there is no active participation of the government and/or various institutional players, the main initiative lies with social actors (such as trade unions, trade associations, etc.) which often, in the absence of co-ordination, orient their schemes to specific sectoral interests. By the same token, the adoption of more or less rigorous tools from the methodological point of view determines the degree of reliability in the results.

The institutional contexts of needs anticipation schemes vary greatly from country to country, oscillating from very structured 'regimes' to situations with a total lack of a structured institutional context, depending on the different weight and role of policies with respect to initial and continuous training, the split of responsibilities between central government and regions, and the role of government and social actors.

Table 7.1 Institutional contexts of the European systems of training needs anticipation

Development stage		
Well structured	**Some structured elements**	**Non-structured**
Denmark (training in alternation; convergence between businesses and employees; 'Training committees')	*Belgium (constitutional reforms aiming towards a federal structure have made it more difficult to develop the two autonomous anticipation systems: Flemish and Walloon)*	*Portugal (interventions lacking co-ordination, funded by EU programmes, with no formal connection or structuring whatsoever)*
Germany (like Denmark; the anticipation system has a direct impact on initial training, while for continuous training the role is left to private institutions)	*Luxembourg (considerable cooperation between government, training institutions and social parties, which has brought about significant changes especially to the initial training system)*	*Greece (like Portugal)*
Britain (the anticipatory system has been widespread since the 1980s with the National Vocational Qualifications, operating both for initial training and continuous training. In 1997 the Qualification and Curriculum Authority-QCA) was established	*Ireland (system of continuous training is in an initial phase; the first active sectors are tourism and agriculture)*	*Austria (the only structures that ensure support to firms undergoing re-organisation are the so-called Technical Assistance Offices)*
The Netherlands (government and social parties involved in Education Industry Committees, which validate occupational profiles and training courses chiefly for initial training)	*Finland (similar to Italy in the growing role of the social parties and the major responsibility of the regions for training; the new central co-ordination body is the Anticipation Group, comprising the Ministries of Education, Labour and Industry, Co-ordination of the Regions and Social Parties)*	
France (similar to Germany and the Netherlands, but central government has greater power; decentralisation of responsibilities both at sectoral and regional levels)	*Sweden (no ministry in charge, but structures responsible to the Ministries of Labour, Industry and Finance which operate at the sectoral level)*	
Spain (central level of action, bilateral initiatives for needs analysis in terms of sectors)	*Italy (concerted action being taken by central government, regions, training institutes and social actors to define a single system of anticipation)*	

Source: Author's elaboration from different sources[1]

Table 7.2 Role of governments in TNA

Government methods and procedures		
One competent authority	**Two or more competent authorities**	**Government with low involvement**
Spain (Ministry of Education for initial training, Ministry of Labour for continuous training)	*Portugal (Competence subdivided between Ministry of Labour and Ministry of Education)*	*Denmark (The social parties play a fundamental role in the anticipation process)*
Britain (Department for Education and Employment DfEE)	*Ireland (Competence subdivided between the Ministry of Labour and Ministry of Education)*	*Belgium (The issues of professional profiles have never been systematically tackled)*
France (Ministry of School and Higher Education for initial training; Ministry of Labour and Social Affairs and sectoral and regional authorities for continuous training)	*Greece (Competence subdivided between the Ministry of Labour and Ministry of Education)*	
Germany (first country to promote the development of training credits; Ministry of Education competent at the federal level for business training, the Länder responsible for training institutes)	*Italy (Competence not subdivided between two institutions at a national level but between the Ministry of Labour and the regional authorities)*	
Luxembourg		
The Netherlands (Ministry of Education)		
Austria (Ministry of Education for initial training, Ministry of Economic Affairs for defining professions)		
Finland (Ministry of Education for initial training)		
Sweden (Ministry of Education for initial training)		

Source: Author's elaboration from different sources[1]

As regards the survey instruments, we may define as formal those tools which are recognised as having a high degree of sophistication, scientifically speaking, which may be used in many sectors and have an actual impact on training courses. By contrast, informal procedures are those that could be defined as formal tools, but which are applied in only one sector, and also informative processes which have not yet been systematically structured and organised (Scazzocchio, 1998).

Table 7.3 Formalisation of survey instruments

Analytical tools: degree of formalisation		
Formal research tools	**Mixed procedures**	**Informal procedures**
Germany	*Ireland*	*Belgium*
The Netherlands	*Greece*	*Portugal*
Britain	*Luxembourg*	*Austria*
France	*Finland*	*Sweden*
Spain	*Denmark*	
	Italy	

Source: Author's elaboration from different sources[1]

Italy's ranking may be represented graphically in relation to three variables identified so as to focus on analytical tools currently being tested.

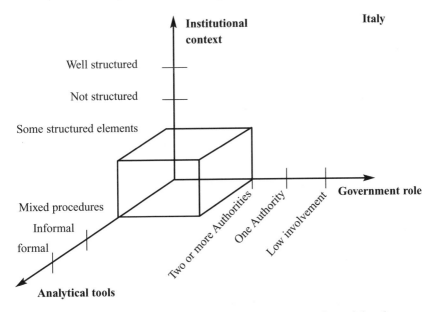

Figure 7.1 Features of the Italian system of training needs anticipation

In Italy, in recent years, those involved in matters concerning the world of employment and training – central and local government, social actors, training institutes – have become convinced of the urgent need to tackle the problem of needs analysis organically. Since the beginning of the 1990s a number of projects have been promoted focussing on training needs analysis, following various approaches, in the absence of a reference framework at a national level. Current developments place Italy among the countries whose analytical tools for anticipating training needs are based on mixed procedures, which are not wholly organised within a single plan at the national level, nor are they left to the initiative of social actors focussing on only one sector of application.

The decentralisation of employment policies to regional and provincial authorities, the expected application of Law 196/97, Art. 17, which remodels the structural characteristics of the training supply and the recent legislation of the European Social Fund, which interprets the aspects of analysis/detection and evaluation as fundamental elements in the process of planning for objectives, have made it imperative, for effective employment and training policy, to disseminate tools to analyse and anticipate professional and training needs[2] within a common framework for all those involved.

A permanent national system for identifying training needs is currently being established, connected to a national observatory on professions. The critical size of the project concerns two levels:

♦ relations and roles of those involved (Ministry of Employment, regional authorities, social actors, ISFOL, associations and institutions);
♦ technical aspects (appropriately structured survey with broad coverage to satisfy training objectives).[3]

The main projects under way,[4] observation of which will, it is hoped, lay the basis for the above-mentioned identification system, are as follows: the OBNF Project (National Bilateral Training Board), the EBNA project (National Bilateral Institute for Arts and Crafts), the EXCELSIOR Information System (System of Chambers of Commerce co-ordinated by the *Unioncamere*).

The Table 7.4 describes the features of the various projects, in terms of: economic sector; firm size; objectives; training subsystem; conceptual categories used; methodologies adopted.

The projects in question have two very different scientific approaches: the first two methods use a qualitative approach, while the Excelsior model is more anchored to quantitative analysis. Both approaches have strengths and weaknesses: in Italy, purely quantitative studies encounter the problem of paucity in the historical series of reliable data regarding training and employment, besides being costly and time-consuming. Exclusively qualitative studies are limited by the fact that they require relatively stable markets to reduce the risk of invalidating the variables assumed to hold for a certain scenario.

The above considerations have led experts from the various parties involved in the projects to postulate both qualitative and quantitative 'corrections'. Moreover, in a subsequent phase, integration between the various models existing would be considered desirable, once they have overcome the experimentation phase.

Table 7.4 Features of the Italian TNA projects

	OBNF	EBNA	EXCELSIOR
SECTOR	Manufacturing	Arts-and-crafts (11 production sectors in various geographical areas)	Industry and services (since 1999 also agriculture, hunting and forestry). Project on a provincial basis
SIZE	Medium-large	Small	Small-medium-large
MAIN OBJECTIVES	1. Define registry of professional profiles 2. Estimate trend in demand for professions on the part of firms 3. Describe the competences of a subset of professional figures	1. Analyse how to create professional competence in arts-and-crafts, indicating the possible processes of acquisition and validation 2. Define models and criteria for analysis, evaluation and certification of competences differentiated between entrepreneurs and skilled workers	1. Construct a predictive information system to analyse short-term labour demand 2. Promote matching between labour demand and supply 3. Provide institutions with information on professional needs for the short/medium term
OTHER OBJECTIVES		1. Identify conditions of irregularity, lack of invoicing and non-regularised labour, and possible legalisation policies	1. Detect the number of job vacancies immediately available (vacancies) 2. Identify the professional needs requirement for non-EU citizens
TRAINING SUBSYSTEM	Training on entry	Continuous training	Training on entry
CONCEPTUAL CATEGORIES	Professional profiles, labour demand, competences	Competences, qualifications, certification	Elementary professions, professional profiles, labour demand
METHODOLOGY	1. Qualitative and negotiated in defining the registry of professions 2. Quantitative in estimating demand forecasts	1. Quantitative in the structural analysis of the arts-and-crafts sector 2. Qualitative in reconstructing components of the competency and pathways to a profession	1. Qualitative and quantitative through the integration of administrative files to create the reference population 2. Extraction of a stratified sample (+ of 100,000 firms) and scaling up of results to the reference population (+ of 1,000,000 firms)

Source: Author's elaboration of ISFOL data

Developing a Strategy: Tools and Techniques for TNA

After outlining European policies in anticipating training needs and comparing Italy's situation with that of other EU countries, the focus is shifted from 'needs analysis' as a tool to support social and employment policies to needs analysis as a phase in the process of designing training programmes.

Flexible and increasingly complex approaches to work demand a strategy for the analysis of training needs rather than a rigid method. This strategy comprises a toolbox of techniques from which one or more techniques can be selected and used. The strategy needs to be part of a continuous process and from time to time it may be necessary to discount some techniques and adopt others as skills requirements and working practices change (Craig, 1994). In other words, the method of analysis that you adopt must be flexible enough to match the flexibility of work patterns.

When developing a strategy for analysing training needs two types of techniques can be applied: information gathering techniques and analysis techniques. The general idea is that one should develop and practise one or more appropriate techniques for the two processes of gathering and analysis.

Before any analysis of training needs can begin, it is necessary to describe clearly the event that has brought about even the slightest hint that training may be needed. This descriptive part uses information gathering techniques. Before choosing the technique(s) for analysis, all relevant information about the event or change has to be gathered. For example, when new technology has to be introduced in a firm, a meeting generally takes place among the top managers in order to highlight all the pros and cons concerning such an innovation. In addition, all the ergonomic implications deriving from the adoption of the technology (that means that a Force Field Analysis and an AET exercise will be conducted) need to be considered. If a new job is required, the selection process will involve a detailed analysis of the functions, tasks and skills necessary to fulfil the role, as well as a parallel session on the single candidate skills (that means that a Job analysis and a Skills analysis will be realised).

The events that might require a TNA can be classified into three groups: first, when people are making a diagnosis for the purpose of making some changes or in order to bring about some improvements in performance at work; second, when training needs are being linked to longer-term strategic planning; finally, when trends of changes are occurring at the level of the entire industry rather than at the level of the single firm. In all cases, it is also important to consider that a single event can assume a different value in particular situations. For example, the introduction of a new job might be a strategic choice made by the firm to anticipate the market or it might represent a necessary step to satisfy its position in the market.

In Table 7.5 different types of techniques are related to typical events. It should be noted that the matrix is not to be treated rigidly; the techniques are linked to the events that seem most appropriate.

Table 7.5 The relation between events and technique use

Events	A	B	C	D	E	F	G	H	I	J
Info gathering technique										
Listening and questioning	X	X	X	X	X	X	X	X	X	X
Critical incident		X	X	X	X	X		X	X	
Brainstorming/brainwriting		X	X						X	X
Survey questionnaire			X		X	X	X	X		X
Analysis technique										
Force Field Analysis		X	X	X	X	X	X	X		X
Delphi		X		X		X				X
Job analysis	X			X	X	X	X	X		
Abilities approach	X			X	X	X	X	X		
AET		X				X	X	X		
Protocol analysis		X								
Repertory grid				X		X			X	
Skills analysis	X	X		X	X	X		X	X	
SWOT	X	X		X	X		X			
Nominal Group			X	X					X	X
Cartoon Storyboard			X			X				X

A. A new Job	**F.** Move to home-based working
B. Introducing new technology	**G.** Move to part-time working
C. Introducing a new working method	**H.** Introducing flexible working
D. Introducing a new process	**I.** Reallocation of responsibilities
E. A move to multiskilling	**J.** Loss of Market share

Source: Adapted from Craig

Focusing our attention on the techniques in Table 7.5, below is their brief explanation, starting from the most commonly used techniques for gathering information:

♦ Listening and questioning. M. Craig (op. cit.) interprets these two skills as real techniques. Active listening, body language, affective questioning are only some of the features that define how the techniques are applied (MacKay, 1980, 1984, 1989; Burley-Allen, 1982; Steil, 1983).
♦ The critical incident technique. Developed by the psychologist John Flanagan (Flanagan, 1954), it aims to reconstruct the behaviours that contribute toward skilled or unskilled performance. It can be used in three ways: face-to-face interviewing, group interview, survey questionnaire (Gerli, 1998).
♦ Brainstorming[5] (Osborn, 1963) and brainwriting (a more anonymous version). The outcome of a session is, or ought to be, a mass of ideas prompted by the question 'How many ways can we think of for...?'. There are around seven or eight variations on this technique (Van Gundy, 1988), but the most appropriate to training needs analysis is to collect written ideas independently and share them

among the group. This is an essential part of the Delphi technique, which is described below.

♦ Survey questionnaire. It is possibly the most widely used and abused method of gathering information. The technique has to be used, if at all, with great caution when collecting information about training needs. Pre-judgement of the outcome is the main disadvantage of using survey questionnaires.

Turning to information analysis, the techniques are:

♦ The force field technique. This technique was initially developed by Kurt Lewin (Majaro, 1988) and provides a simple but effective approach to the initial identifiction of potential training needs. It is used primarily where a change of some kind (in technology, in working practice, in company ownership, etc.) is taking place. A common aspect of change is the conflict between those forces that are driving, or 'for' change and those that are restraining, or 'against', change. The typical tool is the 'force field diagram' that works best when combined with a Delphi-type approach.

♦ The Delphi technique. It was developed by the Rand Organisation in the United States of America, during the early 1950s, primarily as a forecasting tool. It is used in a similar way when applied to the analysis of training needs. The technique is administered by a coordinator and analysis is conducted in seven steps: state the perceived needs, select the managers to involve in the Delphi exercise, design the questionnaire, pilot it, send it with the instructions to managers, analyse the responses and prepare a second questionnaire, analyse the final responses and identify the key areas for training needs, the needs themselves and the preferred way of satisfying those needs. With the Delphi technique one should be able to arrive at a clear consensus about training needs and support.

♦ Job analysis. 'Job' is a complex concept, which is normally analysed by being broken down into identifiable 'chunks'. The most common set of chunks comprises functions, tasks and skills; though each in turn has its own analysis method, they form part of any job analysis technique.

♦ The abilities approach/the skills approach. The different approaches are referred to the level of analysis, when using a job analysis method. Emphasising abilities as opposed to skills can open up a much wider horizon to people in their search for alternative employment.

♦ AET. It is a technique developed in Germany. The name stands for Ergonomic Analysis of Work. It is used in those contexts where ergonomic factors are relevant. Data derived from AET exercises will not be in the form of clear training needs, but will point to areas of concern where implications for training needs exist.

♦ Protocol analysis. The technique was developed to help in the identification of thought processes that lie behind skilled behaviour (Ericsson *et al*, 1985). A protocol can be thought of as a set of rules that we have in our heads for processing 'chunks' of information. Protocol analysis can take one or two forms: concurrent or retrospective according to the time of investigation.

♦ Repertory grid. The technique was developed by George Kelly (Kelly, 1985) and has been used and developed into what has become known as the personal construct theory. The central idea is that we all choose particular ways of constructing the reality around us. The technique is used in TNA to explain differences and similarities in performance at work.

♦ SWOT (*Strengths, Weaknesses, Opportunities, Threats*). The technique has become well known in recent years, and with the now commonly used techniques of brainstorming and survey, is part of a move toward the use of multiple techniques. When people are faced with a new process, new machinery, new marketing strategy or having to adapt methods of working, it can be used to highlight strengths and weaknesses arising. The SWOT analysis is of more benefit when combined with at least one other technique, such as the Delphi method.

♦ The nominal group technique. It involves an exercise not dissimilar to Delphi, but conducted with a group of people gathered together in one place (Scott *et al*,1982). It is effective to assess priorities in training needs. The choice of the ranking criteria is up to the coordinator, whose role is crucial.

♦ Creative techniques.[6] Several techniques are based on creative tools that try to stimulate imaginative capacity of the single person involved in a process of training needs analysis. It is suitable for analysis of the personal training need and to outline a possible career path.

TNA and Key Concepts

In the previous section, a list of techniques was presented and each technique was related to some events. In the development of a TNA strategy it is also necessary to choose the proper 'concept' to adopt to investigate the training needs of the reference context. This choice of the key-concept is driven by factors, such as the training project objectives and the features of the context. The training objectives are the teaching goals to be achieved, meant as the changes in the trainees' professional competence with reference to the organisation's training needs.

Training needs can be grouped into three categories:

♦ training needs for organisational change;
♦ training needs for performance improvement;
♦ training needs for career development.

Within the third category, a dichotomy exists between the concept of career development with reference to the firm and the career development of the single person independently of the firm in which it takes place. A specific objective of training emerges: occupational flexibility, which is the widening of employment possibilities of human resources.

Occupational flexibility is meant as the capacity to activate more complex and articulated organisational behaviour, to work with styles, professional competence, organisational cultures and values different from ours, to interpret at the same time several roles (versatility) (Manara, 1997). This objective is consistent with labour market trends, whose significant features, for training implications, are based on the twin pillars of integration[7] and flexibility[8] (OBNF, op. cit.).

The second factor that determines the key-concept for the investigation is the reference context of professional training, which can be:

♦ the firm (area, function or the entire firm);
♦ the area/territory (local, regional, national, international);
♦ the industry (in the widest sense).

As anticipated, interaction between the objective and context will determine the choice of the concept to adopt in training planning: standard career processes, theoretical knowledge or disciplines, competencies.

If the objective is occupational flexibility it means that the trainee aims to develop a broader professional competence than the current one, in order to apply it in other contexts. It implies that talking of standard career processes is not appropriate, because it is based on the idea of 'fixed positions' meant as a collection of rigid figures within the organisation. It recalls the idea of universal organisations, mechanically transferable, with no consideration of different contexts, needs and personal experience. Organisations in the post-modern society are flat and reticular, reducing their vertical structures and the related rigid professional roles.

Theoretical disciplines tend to make positions consolidated rather than flexible. Such an approach is rigid, binding, centred neither on the persons, nor on the specific firm. In a highly competitive context like the global market, it is necessary to reorganise business processes. Companies need to combine strategic centralisation and operative de-centralisation. The professional competencies required to act in such a turbulent environment derive from technical knowledge related to disciplines in evolution and from the capacity to master emerging branches of knowledge, not yet codified into disciplines.

By contrast, dealing with competencies is an effective way to foster employment flexibility in a training initiative. During the last few years, the concept of competency (see in the next section) has pervaded the managerial, scientific and institutional debate, becoming the crucial and innovative issue of social sciences.

Firstly, competency is in opposition to the concepts of 'position', 'role' and 'qualification', the bulwarks of the *Tayloristic* top-down organisational model. Unlike the first two approaches, competency offers an image of the experience centred on people and on their personal features. The framework in which the relation between individuals and enterprises has developed is changing: from job security (a job for one's whole life) to sustainable employability (lifelong learning in a flexible labour market).

Lifelong learning is meant as a personal right that safeguards access to competencies, which have to be brought to light, stimulated, addressed, preserved and defended from obsolescence. It is widely accepted that the competitive advantage of organisations is determined not anymore by roles or professionals positions, but by human resource quality and that competencies play a crucial role for the achievement of such a quality.

The key words in the 1990s were competencies and competitiveness: being competent to better compete, developing individual competencies to achieve organisational development.

The consistency of a competency approach with a training initiative aiming to foster the job flexibility is even higher when the context of training is an industrial sector, rather than a single firm. Industrial sectors generally consist of differentiated organisations in terms of activities, size and management styles. In the same sector you can find both firms that invest in innovation and firms that still compete basing their strategies on low costs as a weapon for price competition.

Such a heterogeneous environment is the reason why the concept of standard career pathways is not suitable. This approach needs a specific, limited link to a defined context, such as a big firm in which, for example, the administrative officer's career pathway is clear and identifiable. The standard career approach is achieved by matching the behavioural characteristics of the trainee to internal organisational needs, that is to the roles towards which the professional development of human resources is targeted. It is therefore in contrast with the primary objective of occupational flexibility that is often pursued independently of the reference organisation.

The adoption of the concept of theoretical disciplines and knowledge is typical of projects aiming to support internal development processes and performance improvement (Fontana, 1989). It also brings some practical difficulties, multiplying the efforts to organise a rigid training system, because in industry the disciplines of interest are various and multiform, often specialist, and they require the organisation of training for homogeneous groups of trainees. This is the reason why this approach also seems to conflict with the concept of flexibility in training that implies the use of active teaching methodologies, based on the comparison between the different experience and professional backgrounds of trainees.

When one adopts the approach based on competencies, a natural consequence is to explore the context in which the training activity takes place, because competencies are strictly bound with it, they are developed and used in context (the reference organisation). Referring to competencies also implies consideration of *meta-contextual* competencies, those with general characteristics, inter-systemic, expandable in the labour market to increase one's possibility of employment (Camuffo, 1993).[9] Such an approach enables the training organisation to work step by step, from the identification of the basic competencies, ranging from those that define the minimum level of access to the sector, to those necessary for better performance.

The Competency Approaches

The term competency has been defined in the literature from several different points of view. The term has no single widely accepted definition (Strebler *et al*, 1997). Those researching the field, as well as practitioners, have derived several meanings that serve as a focus for their efforts to implement the competency approach in their work. This has produced a multi-faceted concept called competencies. It will be argued that the rationale for the use of competencies will determine the definition given to the term.

A review of the literature showed three main positions taken towards a definition of the term.

Competencies were defined as:

♦ observable performance (Boam *et al*, 1992; Bowden *et al*, 1993);
♦ the standard or quality of the outcome of the person's performance (Rutherford, 1995; Hager *et al*, 1994); or
♦ the underlying attributes of a person (Boyatzis, 1982; Sternberg *et al*, 1990).

Within the first definition the focus, on a person's performance, is concerned with whether they were competent as described in the written standards (Strebler *et al*, op. cit.). The focus is on the output, or task, to be completed.

The second definition sees competency as a standard, or quality of outcome. This definition can be used to pursue gains in productivity or efficiency in the workplace.

The third definition of competency refers to the underlying attributes of a person, such as knowledge, skills or abilities. The use of this definition focuses on the required inputs of individuals in order for them to produce competent performance. This differs from the first two definitions of the competency approach that saw the term as a measure of output of individuals. By describing the existing knowledge, skills or attitudes of competent performers, the inputs needed for the development of a learning program could be defined. Such a syllabus could include the prerequisite knowledge needed in order to perform competently.

Related to the definition of the term is the rationale for using the competency approach. If competency means performance, then the rationale for using the approach is to improve, or in some way change human performance. Where competency means standards or quality of performance, then the rationale is to standardise skills, raise standards, introduce change or set minimum standards of performance.

Where competency means the underlying attributes of individuals, then the rationale is to determine the syllabus or content of learning that will lead to competent performance (Hoffmann, 1999). The third approach seeks to discover not what a person can do, but what they need to know, or what skills or other attributes they need in order to perform at a competent level. Such an analysis provides information on the content of a syllabus for others to emulate their performance.

A table may help explain the differences between each type of approach and the purposes for each (Table 7.6). The input and output on the left of the table refer to the two types of uses of the term competency. The term has been used to refer to both individual and corporate types of competency description. To the right of the table is the purpose for using either an input or an output approach to the definition of competency.

Table 7.6 Competency approaches and purposes

	Individual	Corporate	Purpose
Output	*Performance Standards*	*Perfomance Benchmarks*	Performance-based objectives
Inputs	*Knowledge Skills Abilities*	*Distinctive Strengths*	Subject matter content

TNA in the FIT Project: Approach, Tools and Results

The methodology used for TNA is based on the concept of competency, as described in the previous paragraph within the third approach. The choice of an input based approach (that describes the underlying attributes held that lead to competent performance) rather than an output-based approach (that describes specific performance and standards required) was made by analysing the advantages that each approach gives in each circumstance.

First of all, complex jobs (and 'evolving' jobs, such as those involved in the logistics industry) may best use an input-based approach, while simpler jobs may benefit from an output- based approach, that easily 'measures' performance at work or defines standards for output. Furthermore, the input-based approach, emphasising for each individual the potential and the possibility to do or to be something different, is most suited to a project aiming to foster employment flexibility in the industry. Finally, attention is focussed on the Individual rather than on the Corporation, again because the aim of the project is the pursuit of flexibility, and not necessarily to improve the performance of the single firm. The focus on the distinctive strengths at corporate level might be useful when the aim is to develop training programmes tailored for a specific firm, because the attention on that firm can easily lead to the creation of firm-specific syllabuses.

The tool used, within the competency approach, is the standard professional profile, broken down into *skills*, *knowledge*, and *abilities*. The use of this tool has produced the development of a databank including the standard profiles operating in the reference sector. During the guidance/orientation phase,[10] the profiles outlined were used as 'standards' by which the training-professional gaps of each single participant were identified.

Analysis of the training needs focused on the following types of operators: shipping companies, maritime agencies, forwarders, clearing agents, couriers, hauliers. Shipping companies were analysed in detail. This paper concentrates on the results for this type of operator, with reference to 26 professional profiles outlined as follows:

Table 7.7 Professional profile scheme[11]

Process X	....
Area X	....
Professional profile	....
Role/duties	Role and main tasks performed
Work context	Where the professional activity is performed
Knowledge	
Abilities/Skills	
Crucial relationships	Internal and external relations
Career opportunities	
Access conditions to the profession	
Other information	

The profile articulated in this way comprises several elements that contribute to determining what a specific person in charge of a specific job has to do, and to highlight his/her underlying attributes. The table above shows both 'soft' (abilities, career opportunities, other information, etc.) and 'hard' elements (duties, knowledge, access conditions to the profession, etc.) acting on a precise context that represents the 'background' (work context, crucial relationships, etc.) where the work and liaisons affecting performance are developed.

The professional profiles described in Table 7.7 were the results of a survey conducted through a semi-structured questionnaire in a Delphi approach. The aim of the survey was to gather the greatest amount of information for each profile and then to skim it, via an iterative method, in order to define the profile by using relevant, essential information. The experts concerned in the Delphi exercise, specifically those working in the maritime industry, were involved in a 'top-down' sequence. This first involved those with a strategic and global view of the industry and then those concerned with specific profiles.

No statistical tools were adopted for validation of the results. Instead, analysis was based on a descriptive/qualitative value, comprising at the same time elements of job description and competency. Results were derived using the following steps:

♦ first of all, the global activity performed by shipping companies was broken down into processes, i.e. a 'sequence of flows of inter-related activities aimed at producing a specific output'. During the Delphi exercise the first stage was to find a consensus on the processes that could better depict the whole activity of the shipping companies. Diagrammatically this can be represented by Figure 7.2.

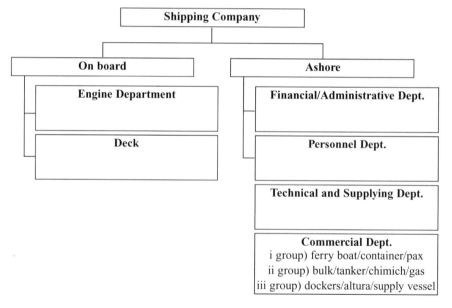

Figure 7.2 Processes in shipping companies

♦ as a second step, within a specific process, a set of *Activity Areas* was identified, each of them meant as the whole set of specific, homogeneous and integrated activities, oriented to the production of a specific output. According to this approach a specific *Activity Area* can be found in different processes, and a specific process can involve different operational professional profiles. Below is an example, referring to the activity areas present in the Personnel Management

Process[12] of shipping companies, in charge of which there are two profiles: the personnel officer and his/her assistant.

Table 7.8 Example of process/activity areas/profiles engaged

Process: Personnel Management	
Area	*Profile engaged*
Area 1: Recruitment and alteration	Personnel officer
Area 2: Seafarers Book-keeping	Personnel officer (*supervision and organisation*)
	Assistant to personnel officer (*operative work*)

♦ in the third stage, each activity area was subdivided into activities referring to the person in charge of the specific activity. In this stage it was necessary to identify the activities and those responsible for each, together with his/her underlying attributes for competent performance (see before). Table 7.9 provides an example of this process, showing all the activities carried out by the two profiles engaged in the process from personnel recruitment, to checking certificates, etc.

Table 7.9 Example of activity areas /elementary activities/profiles involved

Process: Personnel Management		
Activity area	*Elementary activity*	*Profile*
Area 1: Recruitment and alternation	• Co-ordination and control of all the activities related to the management of seafarers • Recruitment of seafarers • Selection of seafarers • Duty rosters • Management of relations with seafarers • Training of officers and crew to familiarise them with the ship, its equipment and the tasks entrusted • Management of relations with maritime agencies and other intermediaries • Control of certificates • Management of provisions	Personnel officer
Area 2: Seafarers Book-keeping	• Compiling of documentation for seafarers alternation • Compiling index-cards for seafarers book-keeping • Compiling index-cards for ashore personnel book-keeping (when missing the Ashore Personnel Department) • Drawing up of documentation for social welfare contributions (INPS/IPSEMA, SSN refunds, CRL, FMN) • Booking office for seafarers embarking or disembarking	Personnel officer (supervision and organisation) Assistant to personnel officer (operative work)

♦ finally, all the information is assembled to depict each professional profile and to reflect the skills/knowledge/abilities required to carry out each activity. In Table 7.10 the profile of the personnel officer is described.

Table 7.10 Example of professional profile

Professional profile	**PERSONNEL OFFICER**
Process	Personnel Management
Area 1, 2	Recruitment and alternation of seafarers / Book-keeping of seafarers
Role and duties	Responsible for the management of seafarers, he/she coordinates the activities carried out in the Personnel Department: recruiting, selection and alternation of seafarers. He/She has discretional power and autonomy in management with respect to the general guidelines given by the shipowners or the executive board. His/Her main duties are: • Coordination and control of all the activities related to the management of seafarers • Recruiting, Selection, Alternation of seafarers • Management of relations with seafarers • Training of officers and crew to familiarise them with the ship, its equipment and the tasks entrusted • Management of relations with maritime agencies and other intermediaries • Control of certificates • Management of provisions
Work context	• Shipping Company or Service Agency for the Maritime Industry • Employee of shipping company or self-employed • Daily work (40 hours/week)
Knowledge	• International regulations (STCW– IMO etc) • International regulations concerning social security, insurance and health • English • Office automation software • Personnel book-keeping software
Abilities/ Skills	• Management of relationships with seafarers • Perception and mediation of seafarers' needs • Satisfying staff requests in accordance with international regulations • Use of personal computers for personnel book-keeping • Negotiation with Trade-Unions and Syndicates • Problem-solving approach to emergencies • Aptitude to organisation and coordination • Curiosity, Capacity to update one's technical knowledge
Crucial relations	• Maritime Agencies • Seafarers (enrolment, embarking, disembarking) • Entrepreneur, executive board • Maritime Book-keeping office • Trade-Unions • Confitarma and Syndicates

Career opportunities	• Emerging possibility of outplacement in service agencies
Access conditions to the profession	• Captain's full certificate of competency (preferably with some months of deck sea-time service as a Ship's Officer) • Considerable experience acquired in the functions of control and coordination
Other information	• For the role played, he/she has to be a person with effective managerial capacity. Generally he/she is called Comandante at 35 years of age, after long periods on board, is bright and inclined for interpersonal relationships. Has to continuously update his/her knowledge of both national and international regulations of maritime labour law

Reading through the description of the profile of the *personnel officer*, for example, it may be noted one is expected to possess a strong background in legal matters, to be able to manage interpersonal relationships and to have been on board for long periods. Indeed, this experience of life on board is often cited as a key factor for competent performance.

The profile can be considered a valid instrument to define the working content for young people interested in working in the industry, or it might direct the professional career pathways of young recruits, not yet aware of their possible alternatives. An interesting aspect that emerged in the profile is the fact that shipping companies now often outsource the management of the crew, especially recruitment and alternation of seafarers. This means that the working context for a *personnel officer* is no longer only the shipping company, but also the emerging service agencies that provide support to shipping firms. This has significantly enhanced job opportunities for those working in human resources within the sector.

For further analysis of labour organisation in shipping, the profiles, read with an integrated perspective, allow comparison among the tasks performed by the different profiles, highlighting overlapping areas of responsibility, or empty spaces, that highlight the need for a different organisation of labour.

Having collected all the information in the field relating to the standard professional profiles, theoretical analysis was carried out, which led to the definition of training modules, through the identification of training areas. This is illustrated in Figure 7.3.

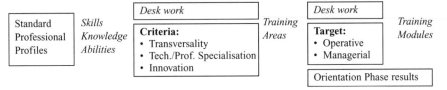

Figure 7.3 From the standard professional profile to training modules

The training areas were derived from the information contained in the variables *knowledge*, *abilities*, and *skills*. In order to highlight the areas of relevance to course planning, the following criteria were chosen:

♦ transversality (knowledge and competencies that widen the range of the employment possibilities, such as information technology, foreign languages, communicative skills, strategic knowledge, etc.);

♦ technical professional specialisation (knowledge and competencies, specific for the transport mode).

A third criteria, that is 'Innovation' (emerging knowledge and competencies in the market not yet codified as specific professional requirements either in quality or quantity,) was used to highlight, among the areas already identified, those which needed particular attention when formalised in teaching modules, such as *safety on board* (Bresciani *et al* op.cit.).

The criteria were chosen with respect to the concept of *competency* that was the keynote for all our work. At the same time, the criteria highlight the *meta-competencies* (behavioural and transversal, those that simply broaden the range of occupational possibilities and that are independent of the context) and the *industry-specific competencies* (theoretical and technical knowledge, those that gain meaning only because performed in that context) (Boyatzis, op.cit.). In addition, much attention was focused on new knowledge and skills because of employment flexibility that requires constant updating and also anticipation of future trends.

The training areas of interest to those involved in shipping that emerged from the work of the panel of experts who identified the priority training areas were as follows: information technology, foreign languages, administration, law, automation, quality, safety and telecommunication. During the orientation phase, the trainees could express their preferences on the training areas. These choices could then be revised or totally changed if a trainee decided during the project to calibrate his/her personal training pathway differently.

The initial choices made by the trainees, guided by coordinators, gave the results presented in Table 7.11, in terms of training needs priorities.

Table 7.11 Priorities in training needs – FIT Project

Training areas	1st choice	2nd choice	3rd choice
Information technology	37%	46%	4%
Foreign languages	47%	10%	2%
Administration/Law		3%	9%
Automation			25%
Quality			20%
Safety	3%	41%	35%
Telecommunication			5%
General interest in training	13%		
	100%	100%	100%

From training areas to training modules a further distinction was made with reference to the different targets: operative staff and managers. Moreover, the interviews organised during the first phase of orientation were intended to gather directly from future trainees significant information for the definition of syllabus contents (a listening and questioning technique was adopted). For example, a clear difference emerged between the recruits and the older officers in their approaches to the study of foreign languages. The former claimed to be able to carry out a conversation in general English but were not familiar with technical language spoken on board. The latter had mastered technical English, but had difficulties when asked to communicate with foreign port authorities, or other organisations, such as institutions in charge of inspections. They needed to improve their general English, to speak with greater fluency. This is why we organised English courses not only at different levels, but also based on different teaching methods (such as simulations for new recruits, conversation and role-playing for officers). At the end of this process, involving both shipping experts and trainers, 27 modules (35 hours each) were planned, during which 74 courses were held.

Some findings on training needs and the culture in the industry are highlighted in the above table. The key areas are information technology and foreign languages (English, both general and technical language). While these skills are generally considered 'basic competencies' for all those trying to enter the labour market, for the professional categories working in shipping (in particular seafarers) they assume the value of very important technical, professional competencies. This is due to the nature of the shipping sector, with its international sphere of action and the spread of information technology that occurred in the 1990s, both of which have affected MET (Maritime Education and Training) priorities.

Likewise, some issues (safety, environment) such as those addressed in relevant international -IMO- instruments and EU directives, have become the core of syllabuses all over Europe. In Italy, where the maritime educational system is still not completely aligned with European requirements, and the entrepreneurial approach towards training is quite reluctant to conceive professional training as a strategic tool to develop human resources, there is less sensitivity to these 'emerging' themes than to 'necessary' competencies (languages and information technology).

Conclusions

In this paper, the concept of training needs analysis was approached from two different points of view: as a priority tool in labour and employment policies and as a key phase in training.

As regards the first approach, the paper set out to evaluate the prospects of the current attempt in Italy to create a permanent system to identify training needs within a European perspective. The current situation, as emerges from the above analysis, is one of transition from a phase of an absolute lack of initiatives (both by institutions and social actors) to a phase of 'proliferating' initiatives, initially ill-connected and often overlapping, more recently co-ordinated by a nation-wide project to institute a permanent national system to identify training needs, connected to a national observatory on the professions.

A second element for reflection concerns the level of formalisation of analytical tools used in different countries. Also in this case, Italy is in a transition phase, during which attempts are being made to build on experience gained through a series of projects at a local and sectoral scale, promoting the integration of the various models used and seeking a synthesis between exclusively quantitative or qualitative approaches.

As regards the second approach, this paper started with the assumption that TNA (*Training Needs Analysis*) has to be based on a series of factors. In the first part a link between events and TNA techniques was established. Basically three types of events generate the need to develop TNA: first, when some changes or improvements in performance have to be brought about; second, the need for longer term strategic planning, finally the need to absorb changes occurring throughout the whole industry. The most common events were related to information gathering techniques and the analysis techniques generally used in TNA.

In the case of the FIT Project, TNA had to be developed within a training initiative aiming to foster employment flexibility in the maritime industry in southern Italy. It was argued that the best approach to develop a TNA is a competency approach, and the suitable methodology could be based on the Standard Professional Profiles engaged in industry. In fact, the need to pursue flexibility led the trainers to exclude, as a reference concept, theoretical disciplines/knowledge and standard careers, both of which are based on the 'position' in the organisation, which is in contrast with the modern flat, reticular organisation. However, the concept of competency conflicts with the concepts of 'position', 'role' and 'qualification' and it inspires lifelong learning policies, which aim to highlight, stimulate, address, preserve and defend individual competencies to enhance employment possibilities.

Of the different definitions of the term competency, we opted for that best suited to define syllabus content, that which interprets competencies as the underlying attributes of a person (Boyatzis, 1982 and Sternberg, 1990). Furthermore, such an input-based approach, emphasising for each individual their potential and the possibility to do or to be something different, is particularly suited to a project aiming to foster employment flexibility in a given industry.

The underlying attributes of the competent performer were related to the *Standard Professional Profiles* operating in the Industry. This methodology, that can be used in every training activity realised in a sectoral context, tries to overcome the problem of the unilateral point of view (i.e. the enterprise or the individual) in training needs analysis. Indeed, the parties involved are entrepreneurs, managers, employees, who are at the same time trainees of the future. The co-determination of syllabus content emerged as an effective way to motivate participants in the training programme.

The standard profile, apart from being the tool used to define training needs, is also a valid instrument to direct young people interested in working in industry towards the content of work, the attitudes and skills to carry it out, and the access conditions to it. Alternatively, it could steer the young in their professional career choices, highlighting the existence of alternative careers not only in the single firm, but in the entire industry.

The profile is also useful for analysing labour organisation in a given industry. In this case, comparison among the activities entrusted to the different profiles can help to highlight overlapping areas of responsibility, or empty spaces, that identify the need for a different organisation of labour.

Notes

1   The overview was based essentially on 'Window on VET systems: EU overview' on www.trainingvillage.gr/etv/vetsystems/overview.

2   ISFOL (National Institute for the Training Development of Workers), *Formazione e Occupazione in Italia e in Europa – Rapporto 1999*, Edizioni F. Angeli, 1999.

3   By general objectives of the project to create the national system to identify needs, we mean: estimation of employment demand for large aggregations; analysis of trends in local production systems and corresponding training needs; certification of skills possessed and professional qualifications achieved by individuals employed or those seeking employment (ISFOL, op. cit.).

4   Other national projects promoted by social actors and trade associations are currently being launched, including the Master Media Project, the Technical Observatory for daily newspapers and information agencies that analyses new professional skills for the information sector and the Chirone Project (renewed) that analyses Italian firms producing and managing public utility network services affected by processes of change.

5   There are four basic rules to be observed when running a brainstorming session: no fixed time limit, all contributions are to be accepted without question, there must be a facilitator who acts to encourage offers of ideas but never questions or changes what has been said, no outside interruptions are allowed.

6   An example of creative technique is the cartoon storyboard technique, that was developed in the United Kingdom, at the Open Business School, in the MBA programme called 'Creative Management'.

7   Integration of phases outside or within the firm, such as 'design teams' in which not only engineering but also marketing, quality, production, purchasing and suppliers converge. Integration of functions (job enhancement, especially the transfer of monitoring tasks to the operator). Integration of duties (broadening of work, versatility).

8   Flexibility is the goal of new philosophies in job organisation, no longer linked to objectives, to the ability to rapidly absorb the variances within and outside the production process, and increasingly less dependent on traditional concepts of performing a task according to set inelastic procedures.

9   The literature on the concept of competency has a dichotomy which is intrinsic to the concept of competency: the tension between its 'contextual' nature and its 'universal' elements. It is widely held that the operative effectiveness of human resource management models based on competencies relies on circumstance. The profiles of competencies identified in firm X are not necessarily effective for firm Y. Processes to identify and formalise competencies depend on the specific organisational context and only appear to be valid within the individual firms in which they are performed (Camuffo, A., 'L'approccio alle risorse umane basato sulle competenze: questioni di teoria e di metodo', *Direzione del Personale*, 1993).

However, this 'contingent' aspect of competencies is interpreted as one of the limits for the application of human resource management methods based on the competencies themselves. To make up for this drawback and provide orientation in the relativism of contexts, meta-contextual models and standardisation of competencies have been, and continue to be, used.

In a managerial framework, we may consider the example of the consultancy firm Hay/McBear. After 20 years of experience in Behavioural Event Interviews conducted world-wide, 21 recurrent competencies were identified which may be linked to higher performance for a broad range of managerial, technical and professional roles in sales and services. These generic competencies are presented in *Competence at work* (1995) by Lyle and Signe Spencer and are grouped into six categories:

1) Creative and operative competency: focus on the result, attention to order, quality and accuracy, spirit of initiative, search for information;

2) Competency of assistance and service: interpersonal sensitivity, customer focus;

3) Competency of influence: persuasiveness and influence, organisational awareness, building of relationships;
4) Managerial competency: development of others, aptitude for command, assertiveness and use of formal power, groupwork and cooperation, group leadership;
5) Cognitive competence: analytical thought, conceptual thought, technical/professional/managerial skills;
6) Competency of personal effectiveness: self-control, self-confidence, flexibility, commitment to the organisation, other features and personal competencies.

Besides inspiring managerial models, the focus on the 'universal' or 'decontextualised' aspects of competencies is the necessary condition for constructing institutional pathways to classify, evaluate and certify competencies, which have also affected Italy in the last few years. Certification in Italy is the subject of an agreement between government and social actors: the problem is how to work together or negotiate models of competency which may be evaluated and certified within a multi-system framework, involving the training sector, labour market and firms.

10 Vocational Guidance was performed in plenary sessions, held before admitting the participant to a specific training course, and in individual interviews during the courses. This enabled the professional profile of each individual participant (knowledge, skills and abilities) to be described and, by comparison with the standard (current or target) profile, led to the identification of the training areas to fill the gap. Moreover, Guidance produced a non-measurable, intangible effect on each individual participant (increase in his/her ability to self-analyse and identify his/her specific professional/training course now, and his/her specific professional career later).

11 Role and duties: everything a person of that profile has to be able to do at work.
Work context: context where the work takes place (type of firm, size, work times and methods, working conditions, tools and equipment used).
Knowledge: notions and theoretical background necessary to work in that position in a specific working context.
Abilities: the innate capacity of human beings to learn and practise skills and knowledge.
Skills: a precise activity that requires both practice and learning for its complete fulfilment.
Crucial relationships: internal and external relations with colleagues, customers, suppliers, etc.
Access conditions to the profession: cultural, professional and legal requisites that regulate the exercise of a specific profession.
Other information: any relevant information that does not fit the scheme.

12 The example was chosen for its simplicity and clarity. The aim is to illustrate the methodology adopted for identification of all the profiles.

References

Barley-Allen, M. (1982), *Listening: the forgotten Skill*, Wiley, Chichester.
Boam, R., and Sparrow, P. (1992), *Designing and achieving Competency*, McGraw-Hill, London.
Bowden, J., and Masters, G. (1993), *Implications for Higher Education of a Competency-Based Approach to Education and Training*, AGPS, Canberra.
Boyatzis, R. (1982), *The Competent Manager. A model for effective performance*, John Wiley & Sons, New York.
Bresciani, P.G., Gatti, M., Tagliaferro, C., Taronna, P. (1992), 'Lineamenti per un modello di rilevazione', *Osservatorio* ISFOL, Nov.-Dec.

Camuffo, A. (1993), 'L'approccio alle risorse umane basato sulle competenze: questioni di teoria e di metodo', *Direzione del Personale*.

Civelli, F., Manara, D. (1997), *Lavorare con le competenze* , Ed. Guerini e Associati, Milan.

Craig, M. (1994), *Analysing Learning Needs*, Gower Publishing Limited, England.

Ericsson, K.A., and Simon, H. (1985), *Protocol Analysis, Verbal Reports as Data*, MIT Press, London.

Flanagan, J.C. (1954), 'The critical incident technique', *The psychological bulletin* 51 (4).

Fontana, F. (1989), *Lo sviluppo del personale*, G. Giappichelli Editore, Turin.

Gerli, F. (1998), 'Fabbisogni: un metodo innovativo', *Cuoa Notizie*, vol. II.

Kelly, G.A. (1985), *The Psychology of personal constructs*, W.W. Norton, New York.

Hager, P., Athanasou, J., and Gonczi, A. (1994), *Assessment-Technical Manual*, AGPS, Canberra.

Hoffmann T. (1999), 'The meaning of competency', *Journal of European Industrial Training*, 23/6, pp. 275-285.

Isfol (1999), *Formazione e occupazione in Italia e in Europa, Rapporto 1999*, Franco Angeli, Milan.

Lipari, D. (1987), *Idee e modelli di progettazione nei processi formativi*, EL Edizioni Lavoro, Rome.

Lyle, A., and Spencer, S. (1995), *Competence at work*.

Mackay, I. (1980), *A guide to Asking Question*, Bacie, London.

Mackay, I. (1984), *A guide to Listening*, Bacie, London.

Mackay, I. (1989), *Expecting Answers*, Bacie, London.

Majaro, S. (1988), *The creative gap*, Longman, London.

Organismo Bilaterale Nazionale Per La Formazione (2000), *Indagine Nazionale sui Fabbisogni formativi*, OBNF, Rome.

Osborn, A.F., (1963), *Applied Imaginations*, Scribner Ed., New York.

Quaglino, G. P. (1985), *Fare formazione*, Il Mulino, Bologna.

Rutherford, P. (1995), *Competency Based Assessment*, Pitman, Melbourne.

Scazzocchio, B. (1998), 'Le analisi dei fabbisogni professionali e di competenze in Italia alla luce delle esperienze nei paesi dell'Unione Europea', *Lavoro e Relazioni Industriali*, Jan–June.

Scott, D., and Deadrick, D. (1982), 'The nominal group technique: applications for training needs assessment', *Training and Development Journal*, June 26-33.

Sternberg, R., and Jolligian, Jr J. (1990), *Competence Considered*, Yale University Press, New Haven, CT.

Strebler, M., Robinson, D., and Heron, P. (1997), *Getting the Best Out of Your Competencies*, Institute of Employment Studies, University of Sussex, Brighton.

Training Village www (1999), *Window on VET systems: EU overview*, www.trainingvillage.gr/etv/vetsystems/overview.

Van Gundy, A.B. (1988), *Techniques of Structured Problem Solving*, Van Nostrand Reinhold, New York.

Chapter 8

Training Evaluation Models: Theory and Applications

Valentina Carbone and Alfonso Morvillo

Introduction

In the field of training the subject of evaluation is one of the most hotly debated issues. Common to all the different reference models and approaches proposed is the focus on the importance and complexity of evaluation within the training process. 'One of the first questions tackled by the continuing debate concerns definition: what is meant by training evaluation and what determines effective training' (Valentini, 2001).

The term 'evaluation' is not synonymous with measuring. Its meaning is much broader, suggesting the idea of giving 'value', that is attributing significance to facts, information and data. By evaluation we mean the activity aiming to express an assessment of the value of a certain training activity. Thus a feature of evaluation is that it associates assessments of value to data obtained from checking as provided for by a system of detection and control, starting from structured and formalised comparison (Amietta and Amietta, 1989).

According to the English definition (Hawes & Bailey, 1985; Rae, 1985), evaluating means acquiring information on the skills levels achieved by the trainees, though in a broader definition, training results may be defined as appreciable changes of any nature and extent produced on a socio-organisational system by training. Evaluating the results therefore means identifying and measuring such changes (Baldwin and Ford, 1988). Effectiveness of a training process is thus measured by identifying and measuring the extent to which the objectives formulated in the project phase have been achieved.

The literature has proposed various interpretations of the dynamics of the relationship between evaluation and training. Some authors, following the 'Hierarchy Theory' (Kirkpatrick, 1967) discussed in this chapter, identify the evaluation of training with the need to record ex-post the effects induced by training. The 'evaluation process' is described as a series of operations whose beginning is fixed in concomitance with the end of training, while 'checking' is defined as the set of actions required to manage the process in its individual phases and follow up on previous phases (Quaglino, 1985). In this case, evaluation constitutes only one tool in checking.

The most recently propounded theories view evaluation as the set of actions and criteria to collect and elaborate critical information that allows decisions to be taken to pursue, stop or change the phases of training (Snyder, Raben et Warr, 1972).

Evaluation of training is thus conceived as an integral part of the training process itself, in that close integration is recognised between the phases of training and those of evaluation. Indeed, what is subject to evaluation is the origin of training (the need), the design structure (aims and methods), the execution (the course) and finally the outcome (learning, behaviour, changes to the context). The various inter-relationships are expressed in the figure below:

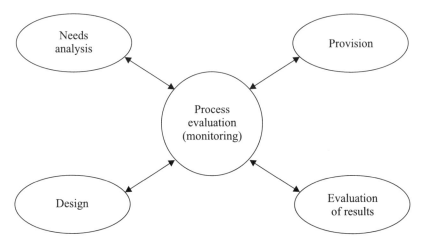

Figure 8.1 Training evaluation

According to the above approach, it is not enough to evaluate only the structure of training, but also the effect of individual and group factors (motivation, expectations, roles, etc.) and that of organisational factors (structure, culture, strategies, etc.) must be analysed. Hence, the effectiveness of the evaluation system and, consequently, that of training itself is inextricably linked to the consistency among the various phases of evaluation and training as well as to their congruence with organisational and environmental variables. There is, therefore, a close inter-relationship between training and evaluation methods. Indeed, there are several evaluation methods or models in training: a suitable evaluation model is chosen according to whether events within or outside the training process are to be understood.

In training adults within the working context, the complexity of evaluation arises from the need to have a multi-polar view of training. The approach to evaluation depends on the system of values assumed as a reference paradigm, which generates the criteria for designing evaluation tools, deciding what to evaluate, and choosing the indicators to be measured. For example, a training course may aim to transfer knowledge or promote teamwork. Clearly, to evaluate achievement of the two different objectives, different models and instruments must be used.

A basic condition for the validity of the evaluation process is that there is good compatibility between expectations, in terms of contents, professional and personal development, role, etc., of all those involved in training. Otherwise, a situation could occur whereby some consider training to be ineffective, there being no consensus on the function such activity should have. Thus, before proceeding to evaluate the effectiveness of training, the compatibility of the aims of the various stakeholders should first be evaluated.

Given the above considerations, this chapter has the following aims:

♦ compare the various conceptual models for evaluation, identifying their strengths and weaknesses;
♦ define an evaluation model consistent with the aims and constraints of the FIT Project;
♦ describe, in critical fashion, operative tools for evaluating training which are reliable, flexible and analytical.

Basic Requirements for a Training Evaluation Model

The success of a training project, whatever the evaluation model adopted, stems from design which allows for certain quality parameters (Vergani, 1991):

♦ *Match*. By 'matching' training we mean training as a service oriented towards the customer and his/her needs. Identification of such needs arises from the integration of what is explicitly stated by the customer and the needs that the trainer perceives.
♦ *Consistency*. By 'consistent' training we mean training which operatively implements its own scientific and pragmatic reference model (Bruscaglioni, 1991). This model underlies the diagnosis involved in the organisation, training needs, objectives and learning methods, as well as the professional skills of training managers and trainers, research that ensures training development, credibility of the methods adopted and the contents proposed.
♦ *Coherence*. Training is 'coherent' if executed systematically and thoroughly in its various components and in its various phases. Such congruence concerns the various operative elements involved in training, the various training phases, the human, technological and structural resources used.
♦ *Circumstance*. This dimension concerns the training location, the relationships formed within the group of participants and flexibility of training times.

In evaluating a training process it is essential to ascertain that these four dimensions are all present and that the evaluation system is structured so as to:

♦ also consider everything that happens before, during and after training, which may affect the result (factors connected to socio-organisational dynamics of the training context);
♦ compare the phenomena in question with the aims defined in the design phase, using the same measurements and tools;
♦ verify compatibility between expectations and objectives of all stakeholders (training managers, trainees, customers) and the general aims of the project.

Evaluation Models: The Various Approaches

Research into training evaluation has gradually identified models which, according to operative contexts, focus attention on one or more aspects of training. Below are listed the models that have been most widely applied in training:

♦ Hamblin's hierarchical model;
♦ pragmatic evaluation;
♦ the contingent approach;
♦ the systemic approach.

Hierarchical theory arose in 1959 with Kirkpatrick and was subsequently researched and modified by Hamblin. This is still considered one of the most well-established theories in the field of evaluation of training results. According to Kirkpatrick's model, the results of training are achieved at four distinct levels:

♦ the level of reactions, in which the main aim is to measure the degree of satisfaction of the participants with the training experience. For such measurements, a quality scale is used (poor, fair, good, excellent) that participants have to assign to the various features of the course during the closing phase of the training course;
♦ the level of learning, in which the task of the evaluator is to measure the knowledge, techniques and skills that have been acquired by each trainee. What is of interest is the difference between pre-course and post-course values;
♦ the level of behaviour, in which the task of the evaluator or of the 'control group', consisting of experts with different skills (trainers, psychologists and organisational analysts), is to find out how training has changed the way the trainees work. Evaluation in this phase undoubtedly requires a greater effort than in the above two levels, in that many factors come into play, such as the organisational climate, motivation, predisposition to change but especially the capacity to transfer into the workplace what has been learnt during the lesson or structured discussion in the classroom;
♦ the level of directly observable results in the organisation as a whole. It is at this level that the model has evolved thanks to Hamblin's work, according to whom the performance of an organisation may be improved by both acting on organisational variables, and on management variables consisting of economic results expressible in monetary terms, such as sales, costs and profitability. The substantial difference between Hamblin and Kirkpatrick lies in the fact that while for the latter any changes recorded ex post at the organisational level cannot be attributed to the training process, in Hamblin's model organisational changes are directly correlated with training. Moreover, for Hamblin, the choice of results to be considered is made while objectives are defined, in the phase of training needs analysis, and not when training has finished. Evolution of the hierarchical model has thus been marked by a shift from ex-post measurement of results for various hierarchical levels, to the definition *ex ante* of training objectives for each level of the process.

In brief, Hamblin's approach may be said to be based on the following assumptions:

♦ there are various types of training objectives, to each of which correspond as many different results;
♦ training may be evaluated by examining how much is transferred by the trainees to the workplace, rather than only in terms of an increase in their knowledge and a change in attitudes.

By classifying the various types of results, a logical cause-effect sequence may be constructed in which training causes reactions in participants that lead to learning, which in turn produces changes to behaviour in the workplace. Such changes have effects upon the functioning of the socio-organisational system and are the ultimate goal of training (see Figure 8.2).

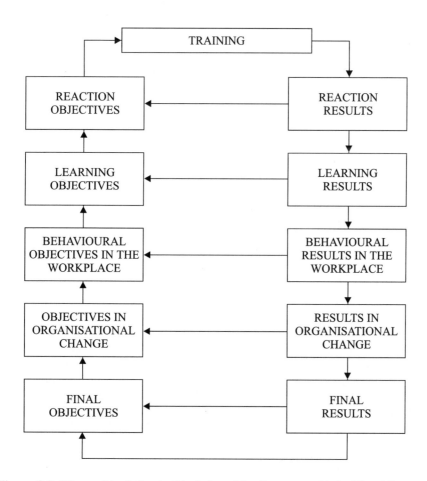

Figure 8.2 Hierarchical chart of training objectives – results by Hamblin (Hamblin, 1974)

Pragmatic evaluation arises from the conviction that more sophisticated procedures to evaluate results are very costly, rather impracticable and unsuited to business situations. Supporters of this theory strongly criticise the hierarchical approach, stating that it is excessively oriented to the past, strongly focused on methodological problems while ignoring those relating to content and, lastly, an approach that undervalues the importance of decisions on the use of information gathered during evaluation (Connolly, 1983).

The pragmatic approach is essentially based on setting up evaluation tools and the subsequent processing of gathered data, minimising both resources and time. The choice of techniques will depend on some combination of methodological and pragmatic questions, and there is a need to settle for 'sensible' evaluation – one cannot measure the impact of management training on the whole organisation but must make some compromises. Questionnaires, surveys and structured interviews should be carefully designed and field-tested to ensure that worthwhile information is received (Foxon, 1986).

The literature review relating to this approach confirms the belief of Morris (1984) that evaluation is regarded by most practitioners as desirable in principle, but difficult in practice. It also highlights the lack of well written and documented articles for practitioners to learn from.

An example of the pragmatic approach is that proposed by Connolly which consists in asking trainees what they have learnt during training and how they have been able to use the information in the workplace. The evaluation process entails the preparation of analytical tools, making the trainees aware of the aims of evaluation, gathering and then processing data as well as preparing a brief report with operative proposals.

The *contingent approach* (Clement and Aranda, 1984) consists in identifying several context variables which decisively affect the success or failure of a training programme. According to this model, evaluation must consider variables other than just the training course, e.g., organisational setting within which the manager seeks to use training, unique characteristics of the manager to be trained, nature of the organisational problem to be solved by training. The shortcoming of the approach lies in the partial nature of results as the consistency of the organisational context is a necessary but not sufficient condition for training to provide utility from the standpoint of the firm's economy.

The *systemic approach* is characterised by an evaluation process which goes well beyond the simple need to monitor both on the part of programme trainers and trainees. Indeed, if besides these two main stakeholders in the training process we also consider other stakeholders, such as firms and organisations responsible for managing the training system, with their own evaluation needs, then the pressure on the evaluation process increases and assumes broader significance.

One could go further to say that although the most easily recordable assessment is that made by trainees using questionnaires or evaluation forms, this evaluation is limited to the relationship between trainer and trainee and to classroom dynamics. However, this evaluation system only serves to reconfirm at each stage the projects and trainers that achieve high degrees of satisfaction, accelerating the involution process of the training system towards a perverse spiral of conforming with the demands of individuals who should instead be stimulated to make continuous changes.

Therefore, it is fundamental to insert training into a structural context of the organisation and verify its results, monitoring the following three systems:

♦ the elements of the training programme at the time of implementation: trainers, previous experience of trainees, learning processes, role orientations and behaviour, specific contents, etc.;
♦ elements peculiar to the individual: aptitude in applying new skills, conceptual frameworks of reference, etc.;
♦ the structural subsystem which contains the individual and his/her role: stimulus to change, innovative information, etc.

The originality of this approach lies in the way relationships are identified between training, the individual and the organisation in terms not of cause-effect but input-output.

It was Warr, in 1972, who produced the first organic formulation of the systemic evaluation model. It is a continuous process, characterised by the typical control mechanism based on action-feedback-decision-action. Warr thus proposes that the evaluation process be organised into five steps (see Figure 8.3):

1. *Context evaluation.* Such evaluation refers to the starting phase of training, and especially concerns needs analysis, during which we must assess how much space to devote to training compared with other interventions and record the needs and expectations of the users of this service. Attention is focused on the organisational conditions on which training will impact. The aim is to discover the possible discrepancies between the current state of the situation and the target state, suggesting change-oriented action.

2. *Input evaluation.* Such evaluation aims to construct the database needed for decisions concerning training design in terms of teaching resources, techniques, methods and organisation. At the same time, the decision is made as to which model to adopt for evaluating the results, choosing the information gathering method consistent with either type of training objective: in practice, in this phase a formalised test procedure is constructed to evaluate the causal connections between action and results. An inventory is then made of available resources and the operative strategies adopted in human resource management, with a view to selecting projects that best fit the need to change identified in the previous phase. In this phase, training programme objectives are defined and training contents and methods chosen.

3. *Evaluation of implementation.* This third step consists in continuous monitoring of training under way to detect possible factors that impede the achievement of set objectives or any shortcomings in training design so as to make necessary changes without having to wait until the end of the training course.

4. *Evaluation of results.* Verification a *posteriori* of results is the fourth and last step in the evaluation process. In this context a distinction should be made between direct results, that is those that can be verified immediately at the end of the course, and indirect results, that is those concerning the behaviour of the trainees in the workplace and the overall functioning of the organisation. In this phase an overall assessment is formulated from the information processed in the preceding phases.

5. *Prospective evaluation*. In this phase the generalisation of the results is evaluated, as well as the possible re-proposal of the project in the light of new requirements for organisational change. The possible alternatives include changes to the training programme, its total transformation or the shelving of the project itself.

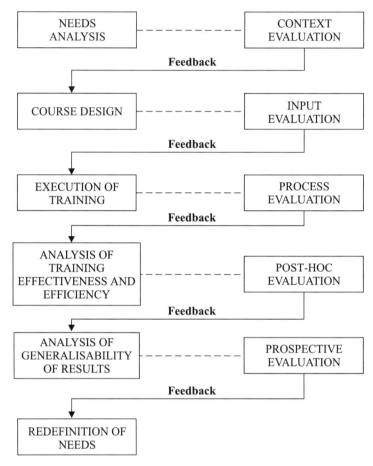

Figure 8.3 The systemic evaluation model (Warr, 1972)

A major feature of the model proposed by Warr consists in the continuous control mechanisms that form the backbone of evaluation, a dynamic process running parallel to the training process. The structure of the evaluation process is thus characterised by a sequence of procedures of information gathering, analysis and feedback for the stakeholders.

The models described above attribute different importance to the following characteristics: self-evaluation, standardisation of tools used, performance analysis, focus on subjectivity, and follow-up.

♦ *Self-evaluation.* The informative potential produced by self-evaluation procedures may be associated to biases due to participant perception, caused by giving opinions in the heat of the moment. The basic lacuna is the lack of objectivity in recording information.
♦ *Standardisation of evaluation tools used.* The customary use of standard tools characterises most post-course approaches to evaluation. Standardisation of evaluation tools on the one hand ensures easy management of information and comparability of results, while it makes it difficult to detect elements which are unforeseen during the design of the tools themselves.
♦ *Performance analysis.* Performance analysis, according to the principle that directly correlates training and results in the workplace, allows the degree of training effectiveness to be measured ex-post.
♦ *Focus on subjectivity.* Evaluation strategies focusing on subjectivity attribute a key role to the trainee and are a feature of action designed to develop individual professional skills. They highlight a contradiction between emphasis on the inherent need of any evaluation to be objective and explicit abandonment of the same objectivity.
♦ *Follow-up dynamics.* The greater or lesser attention paid to follow-up dynamics highlights the importance ascribed to organisational and, more generally, environmental factors, for consolidating the effects of training. One of the ways to achieve such dynamics is the resumption of training after a period of time, which allows us to ascertain the levels of learning acquired by participants who are reintroduced into various working contexts.

Once the most appropriate evaluation model has been chosen, on the basis of the above features (see alsoTable 8.1), the following factors also need to be analysed:

♦ the actual feasibility of evaluation, that is the availability of resources in terms of quantity and quality (human resources, time, financial resources, equipment, access to key information);
♦ the level of evaluation on which to focus (individual, role, organisation, socio-economic context);
♦ the breadth, that is the size of the sample to be evaluated and the time horizon;
♦ attribution of authority and responsibility for evaluation;
♦ data sources;
♦ planning of data collection (recording times, control groups, size and composition of samples, data processing, use of alternative instruments);
♦ methods for analysing and disseminating the evaluation results, to be chosen so that the information is understandable, detailed and accurate in relation to the various users;
♦ actual applicability of methods deemed optimal;
♦ availability of sufficient time.

Table 8.1 Classification of evaluation models

Model	Features														
	Emphasis on self-valuation			Standardisation of tools			Performance analysis			Focus on subjectivity			Attention to follow-up dynamics		
	High	Med.	Low	High	Med.	Low	High	Med.	Low	High	Med.	Low	High	Med.	Low
Hierarchical model		✓				✓	✓					✓		✓	
Pragmatic evaluation	✓				✓				✓	✓					✓
Contingent approach			✓	✓					✓		✓				✓
Systemic approach		✓			✓			✓			✓		✓		

Evaluation Techniques

In defining the training evaluation system we must pay particular attention to techniques to apply in relation to the various aspects of the evaluation problem in question.

Table 8.2 illustrates the classification of the most commonly used evaluation techniques proposed by Salinger and Deming (1982) which relates such techniques to the main evaluation problems among the many hitherto studied in the literature.

Table 8.2 Main evaluation techniques (Salinger and Deming, 1982)

Evaluation problem	Evaluation technique
• To what extent does training produce appropriate learning?	• Control group with different treatment
• To what extent is learning transferred to the workplace?	• Modified "critical incident" method • Performance analysis
• To what extent is the level of knowledge and operative skills maintained in time?	• Evaluation based on time series
• Does the value of improved trainee performance equal or exceed the cost of training?	• Cost-benefit analysis

Each of the above evaluation techniques raises some critical questions which are worth noting:

♦ measuring the results of training by using *control groups* requires particular attention in selecting the components of the group itself. The key features of the components must coincide with, and be proportionate to, those of the class.

Moreover, the choice of measuring times is of fundamental importance. To avoid bias, the survey should be carried out at the same time on all the sample elements. Finally, in analysing the results due consideration should be paid to the so-called 'Hawthorne effect' concerning the difficulty of interviewees in verbally expressing what they think or feel (Draper, 2001).

The most common evaluation procedures using control groups generally fall within the following categories, with slight variation possibilities within each category:

– control groups with pre-training and post-training measurement;
– control groups with only post-training measurement;
– pre-training and post-training measurement of various groups at different times.

♦ The *critical incident method* (see Chapter 7) is severely affected by the subjective view of the interviewee and his/her real capacity to identify situations and moments in which his/her work benefited from what was learnt during training. Moreover, what is stated by the interviewee may be greatly influenced by the Hawthorne effect.

♦ The method based on *measuring performance* raises a series of problems connected with clearly identifying links between what is learnt on the course and improvement in operative performance, which may actually depend on a series of factors which are totally or partially independent of the training itself.

♦ *Time series evaluation*, whatever the method chosen to record data, has typical problems of managing, in time, a considerable body of data.

♦ *Cost-benefit analysis* applied to training processes is problematic, not so much in terms of cost valuation (structural costs, planning costs, materials, tuition, participants, equipment, logistics, etc.) which is fairly straightforward and exhaustive, but especially in evaluating benefits, which never perfectly match the objectives of the same training project. Such objectives may never be completely achieved, while other unforeseen positive effects may well affect those involved in the training project. Until now, all the evaluation models developed which are based on cost-benefit analysis have actually focused only on costs and only allow the economic efficiency of management to be assessed, but not the effectiveness of training.

In more general terms, the techniques described have a limitation in common: they are of a mainly deterministic nature, which does not sufficiently highlight the multi-causality of the phenomena in question. Furthermore, even where the above problem has been emphasised, no useful suggestion has been proposed to identify factors which are complementary to training that could account for possible differences between measurements carried out at different times or on different participants. Generally no organic or integrated view of the evaluation process is thus adopted.

Evaluation Tools

Evaluation of training requires an interdisciplinary approach that uses tools belonging to both the social sciences and the so-called 'exact sciences'. The type of data in question is mostly linked to the type of training intervention studied. However, there are some data categories[1] that recur in all training situations:

♦ data from global analysis of the social, organisational and cultural system to which the trainees belong;
♦ data from analysis of the tasks performed by the trainees and analysis of future assignments;
♦ data from qualitative analysis of the human factor, motivational and psychological phenomena which give rise to behaviours, etc.

To obtain such data three basic measuring tools can be used: direct observation, questionnaires and tests.

Observation-based measurements are potentially better than measurements of objective performance, in that they identify with greater certainty the real reasons for a given final result and, as they are non-intrusive measurements, they are free from the artificial psychological effect peculiar to structured evaluation systems. For example, in the case of groupwork, observation of group dynamics made by the tutor during classwork allows us to acquire information without negatively affecting the spontaneous reactions of the trainees; by contrast, administering structured tests may create stress in the trainees which alters their performance, thereby invalidating learning evaluation. However, measurements based on observation have certain difficulties connected with the standardisation and treatment of data.

Questionnaires and structured tests with evaluation scales are normally used to evaluate the direct results of training in terms of course satisfaction and trainee learning levels. Such tools may be used for quantitative elaboration with a view to obtaining a summary of how the course went. Tests, which have to be constructed specifically for each training project, may be useful sources of data, provided that the validity and the reliability of the measurements are guaranteed by experts in the subjects forming the training programme. Such data should be gathered immediately after the end of each module. However, ex-post evaluation can also be carried out both at the end of the course and after a certain period of time. Indeed, evaluation is often modified especially as regards aspects concerning course satisfaction.

A questionnaire to discern course satisfaction should first include organisational aspects, then a part covering the distribution of time among the various subjects, a third section on the course's future professional usefulness and a final part covering course contents in terms of whether or not they matched expectations.

When to Evaluate

From the operational point of view, three different times in the evaluation process may be distinguished: pre-course, while-course and post-course evaluation.

♦ *Pre-course evaluation* aims to ascertain, prior to investing resources in the concrete implementation of a training course, the suitability of the investment choice in question. Such evaluation generally focuses on different aspects: method of training needs analysis, suitability, consistency of training goals with the training context, topicality and transferibility of the training contents into the work place, course length, methods and organisation.
♦ *While-course evaluation* aims to make available useful information in order to

intervene in the training process under way by modifying it and/or improving it before it finishes. This focuses mainly on: working methods, trainer performance, calibration of the teaching programme according to trainee characteristics, trainee participation and involvement, teaching materials and aids used, group atmosphere, logistical conditions, in relation to the design parameters.

♦ *Post-course evaluation* has the purpose of checking the execution of the process and the results of short-, medium- and long-term training, according to criteria of effectiveness, efficiency, relevance and transferibility. The essential aims thereby are to reconstruct the process as carried out and compare it with what was actually planned. In particular it analyses: the degree to which training objectives are achieved, the curricula/experience of trainees, the extent to which the skills acquired are actually applied in the productive context, the variation in parameters of performance and functioning upon which training was expected to impact, as well as possible unexpected effects.

The Actors in Evaluation

Interpretation of evaluation as an integral part of the training process suggests that the various actors involved should also be protagonists in the evaluation process.

The training managers, in the broadest sense as designers and those in charge of training, are interested in evaluating the results of training both to confirm the validity of their work and to have an objective reference according to which changes can be made to the programme of subsequent training courses.

The trainers are more interested in evaluating the actual teaching situation, so as to obtain both useful suggestions for improving teaching material supplied, classroom management times and techniques, and to gain new professional stimuli from the results of evaluation.

The trainees, in their two-fold position as the subject/object of evaluation, hold the largest body of information. For them, evaluation may also serve to reinforce learning, highlighting positive results or lacunae to be filled.

Lastly, we should not overlook the interest that some *external stakeholders* (employers, trade unions and professional associations, central and local government, etc.) may take in the results of the evaluation process. They use such results as a tool to make a series of decisions that will have both weight and importance going far beyond the individual training project.

Evaluation in the FIT Project

Analysis of the evaluation models illustrated in this chapter highlights the approach which best suited the characteristics and structure of the training project in question. Of the models examined, the one which best meets the need for information and evaluation of a complex training project, such as the FIT, is undoubtedly the systemic model. Indeed, it is the only model which makes a well-balanced use of evaluation and self-evaluation systems, in relation to trainer, tutor and trainee perceptions, and continuously monitors the training process.

The systemic model lays the stress on performance analysis and follow-up dynamics. The approach is particularly suitable for evaluating the effectiveness of a project like FIT, aiming to transfer and enhance useful skills for the professional development of the trainees. Measuring the impact of training in the workplace provides useful information to improve and redefine the teaching methods used and the contents conveyed in projects of this nature. Lastly, the systemic model focuses greatly on subjectivity. This is consistent with the project's main aim to promote occupational flexibility. Hence the model in question allows individual needs and the relative satisfaction level to be discerned, favouring the formation of personalised training paths and avoiding the implementation of standardised processes that may prove somewhat ineffective.

From the viewpoint of the training manager, evaluation improves the use of resources, specialises training in its contents and leads to the professional growth of its trainers. It is thus worth carrying out a thorough analysis of the training process to be implemented. Indeed, it is difficult to improve or repeat a process without having analysed it and understood it in depth. The *mapping process* (see Figure 8.4) consists in gathering, organising, interpreting and documenting the phases of a process through graphic or descriptive representation. The Mapping Process:

♦ increases the level of understanding of the processes and functions;
♦ facilitates the understanding of resource allocation criteria within such processes;
♦ allows the design of transactional flows for the various procedures;
♦ constitutes a useful tool for learning procedures;
♦ enhances the awareness of one's own role in the flow on the part of each actor;
♦ facilitates the use of appropriate tools to monitor the process itself.

By process we mean a coordinated 'flow' of correlated activities (input/output) which, through the direct/indirect involvement of units both within and outside the organisation and resource use, aims to achieve objectives/results characterised by 'continuity' and/or cyclicity.

Under this meaning, each training scheme may be represented as a process.

To interpret the scheme illustrating the process in question, we need to highlight the starting-point (input), the arrival (output) and each point in between that enabled the main objective of the monitoring and evaluation system to be achieved, namely creating quality, hence guaranteeing a quality service/product. The project's starting-point is previous experience in training in the transport sector,[2] both on a national and regional level (Campania). Initiatives in the field show that there is a latent training need which is not yet well-defined. There appears to be a general need for employment categories to adapt to new logistical characteristics which have evolved from a straightforward service to a service with immense added value, requiring versatile, integrated skills.

The FIT project falls within the framework of initiatives that seek to define, for each job profile, the knowledge, skills and aptitudes required to ensure that the labour supply effectively satisfies new demands (output of the project: gap reduction between demand and supply).

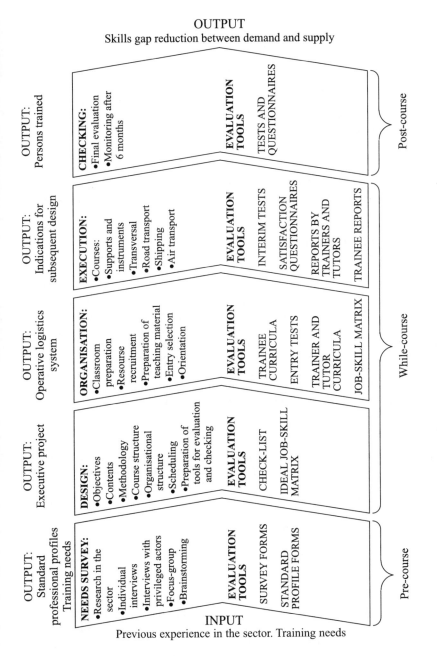

Figure 8.4 The mapping process of Evaluation-FIT Project

To monitor the whole process in all its various phases, a series of evaluation activities were conducted using specific analytical tools.

Below is a description and critical evaluation of some of such tools. The tools were chosen either according to the importance of the training areas concerned or the innovative aspect from a methodological point of view. The strength of the evaluation system adopted by the FIT project lies in the organic nature of the various phases and in the complementary nature of the tools, designed to analyse not only planning and organisational features, but also those more strictly connected to learning and its effects in the workplace.

Evaluation and Needs Survey

In the trainee needs survey phase, thanks to the support of sectoral insiders, supplied through the focus groups, as well as the training course recipients, obtained by individual interviews, two evaluation tools were drawn up: forms that outline the standard profile of recipients (see Chapter 7) and forms to record the educational-employment curriculum of the trainees.

The form to record the educational-employment curriculum of trainees (see Table 8.3) consisted of four areas: an area giving personal information, a second area concerning trainee education up to project execution, a third area representing the employment situation of the trainee, and a fourth area focussing on trainee expectations in terms of subject areas of interest and preferential training modules.

With the support of this form, each user could be guided in defining his/her own ideal training plan, consistent with specific personal/professional needs. Drawing up the personalised training plan, consisting of a set of training modules that each user intended to follow, was decisive for the phase of executive design, during which priority was given to some subject areas rather than others, and in some cases, new modules were planned that were not envisaged in the original project.

Evaluation and Design

Analysis of information recorded during the needs survey was followed by the design phase and hence the definition of objectives, contents, methodology, structure and duration of the training course. To monitor the design phase, a check-list was used (see Table 8.4). The list indicates a series of crucial elements for sound training design, organised into three areas: executive design, partners involved and organisational abilities of the training manager concerned. Clear identification of these elements and their constant monitoring during the project are essential elements for effective project management.

Evaluation and Organisation

Once the executive project was set up, we proceeded to the organisational phase of training during which resources (trainers and tutors) were engaged according to their curricula. Moreover, trainees were thoroughly evaluated. In particular, the skills of the participants were evaluated not only on the basis of data emerging from individual interviews, and from forms recording educational and occupational curricula, but also with appropriate entry tests. This information allowed us to identify the actual profile of participants and to compare it to the ideal profile, derived from the phase of training needs analysis, by transferring the relevant information to the Job-Skill matrix. This matrix permits visual identification of the gaps in terms of skills and knowledge for each participant *vis-à-vis* the characteristics of the ideal profile. This is illustrated by the following table showing the real profile of each personnel officer compared to his/her ideal profile. In the table, grey lines highlight a wider gap between ideal/real knowledge and skills.

Table 8.3 Data collection

Personal information	First name and surname	
	Address	
	Telephone	
	Date of birth	
	Marital status	
Education	School type	
	Training	
Employment	Previous work experience	Firm
		Tasks
	Current employment	Firm
		Tasks
	Acquired knowledge	
	Acquired skills	
Motivations and expectations	Training modules chosen	
	Training areas of interest	

Table 8.4 Check-list for training course design

CHECK-LIST	NOTES
Executive design	
• Are there other training providers supplying similar activites?	
• How can demand for this need be stimulated?	
• Are the tools adopted to evaluate training methods appropriate?	
• Are customers/end-users involved in evaluating training needs?	
• ...	
Potential project partners	
• Who are the potential partners in the project (social partners, universities, research centres, training associations)?	
• Are relations under way with: the market (customers, other suppliers, funding institutions) experts?	
• ...	
Ability to execute the course	
• In what way does the project link with previous experience?	
• Are competent, qualified trainers available for the project?	
• Are the available premises and equipment appropriate?	
• Is the project feasible from the economic point of view?	
• Are quality assurance procedures well-defined, appropriate and feasible?	
• Is the organisation able to run the project?	
• Have potential participants received information material?	
• ...	

For example, from the previous table, the widest gaps for the trainee may be highlighted: they concern computer skills for on-board book-keeping, knowledge of safety standards and command of English. The trainee was encouraged to participate in training modules related to such themes, in order to plug the gap and acquire the skills required by the labour market.

Evaluation and Execution

After the organisational phase, the execution phase of the training courses was conducted, which was monitored by interim tests, satisfaction questionnaires, trainers' reports on trainees and trainees' reports on trainers and tutors.

Training effectiveness was evaluated during the courses by using a series of tools. For each subject covered, the trainees were asked to undergo a series of tests to evaluate the skills acquired. Depending on the subject taught, the tests were administered either as questions with open responses or in multiple choice format, as simulations or as business games. The results were discussed with the trainers and tutors.

The trainees were asked to express their opinion on the quality of each training module, evaluating the trainer, contents and teaching aids by filling in a form (see Table 8.6). In this form, the trainees were also asked to evaluate their own skills level before and after the course.

Table 8.5 Example job-skill matrix (real/ideal profile): Personnel Officer

Skill/knowledge/attitudes	*Value*									
	1	2	3	4	5	6	7	8	9	10
Ability to manage relations with crew							O			X
Ability to perceive and reconcile the needs of the crew							X O			
Ability to satisfy needs of the crew compatibly with opportunities provided by international legislation							O	X		
Ability to use a personal computer for on-board book-keeping	O							X		
Ability to negotiate with trade unions and professional associations							O	X		
Ability to manage emergencies with a problem-solving approach							O			X
Skills as organiser and coordinator								O		X
Professional curiosity and ability to self-update							X	O		
Knowledge of international maritime law (STCW – IMO etc.)								O	X	
Knowledge of safety standards				O					X	
Command of English			O					X		
Knowledge of the ship and its equipment									X	O
Administrative skills							X	O		
Legend: X Ideal profile O Real profile										

These data were compared with the results of interim tests so as to reach an evaluation of training effectiveness that reconciles the perceptions of trainers and trainees.

With regard to aspects more strictly linked to trainee performance, the assessments of tutors and trainers were considered on the basis of what was reported in the evaluation forms. Both parties were asked to use one of the grades (Poor, Fair, Good or Excellent) to evaluate the following three features for each trainee:

To be assessed by the tutor
♦ Communication skills
♦ Interaction skills
♦ Degree of participation

To be assessed by the trainer
♦ Analytical skills
♦ Summarising skills
♦ Evaluation skills

Use of such analytical tools is fundamental. They allow the training process to be modified while under way, so as to meet training aims more effectively and provide a quality service.

Table 8.6 FIT course evaluation form

Course: _____

Trainer: _____

Edition code: _____

EVALUATION ITEMS	Excellent	Good	Fair	Poor
A-THE TRAINER				
Ability to convey subject contents				
Level of classroom interaction				
Attention to trainee learning needs				
B-SUBJECT				
Appropriacy of contents to learning objectives				
Value of practical applications for learning purposes				
C-TEACHING AIDS				
Appropriacy of teaching materials to course contents **(if distributed)**				
D-OVERALL EVALUATION				
E-HOW DO YOU RATE YOUR KNOWLEDGE OF THE SUBJECT				
BEFORE THE COURSE				
AFTER THE COURSE				
F-ANY FURTHER SUGGESTIONS				

Evaluation and Checking

A rapid way to have an idea of possible similarities that may be detected among the courses starting from overall observation of the variables measured may be provided by Automatic Classification Techniques. Such techniques are usually employed at the end of the whole training project, considering the units (in our case the individual courses) as points in space with as many dimensions as there are variables observed (in our case the average evaluations of the courses held on different aspects in question). They group together all the points detected in a certain number of 'cluster' differentiated by the various values assumed.

An interesting feature of Automatic Classification Techniques, especially of so-called hierarchical techniques, lies in the fact that the desired number of groups does not have to be established in advance but may be obtained by observing the classification tree, having reported the points observed on the x-axis, and on the y-axis the distances at which they progressively cluster. In our case the classification tree was as follows:

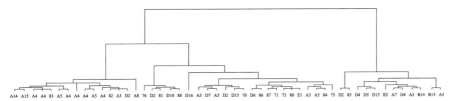

Figure 8.5 The classification tree

Five classes were thereby defined, with averages within each group being reported and compared with general averages. A quantity, or test value, was also defined: the more the corresponding variable characterises the group, the more the quantity increases in absolute terms.

Observation of these test values allows definition of various classes. The first class, which includes 25% of the courses, is characterised by the fact that it recorded higher averages as regards trainer evaluation (ability to convey contents, classroom interaction and attention to learning) but also regarding the subject (consistency of contents/objectives, value of applications). It is also the group where preparation both before and after the course was evaluated slightly below average by the trainees themselves. The overwhelming majority (82%) of the courses in this class belong to the 'Supports and Tools' group.

Such results may be explained by the fact that the Supports and Tools courses allowed the trainees to plug some structural lacunae (poor knowledge of foreign languages, computer illiteracy, etc.) which place the person concerned at a disadvantage with colleagues and employers, and more generally, with the basic professional skills required by the labour market. Moreover, such course types are those which are more consistent with the general objectives of the FIT project, such as pursuit of occupational flexibility, stimulus for self-learning skills and development of an entrepreneurial culture to training.

By contrast, the second class includes the courses for which trainees declared an above average overall preparation, both before and after the course, and for which the same students particularly appreciated the part related to practical applications and teaching material supplied. Most of such courses (70%) are in the 'Shipping group'. Those belonging to the shipping sector, especially seafarers, showed a higher degree of interest and performance than the other categories. One of the explanations for such better 'performance' lies in the very structure of the labour market for seafarers, which is very flexible and complex, and favours an entrepreneurial approach to training on the part of operators. However, where the labour market has career paths which are stable and linear (Port Authority employees), greater problems are encountered in involving trainees and in trainee performance, which is consistent with a view of alienation and 'intolerance' *vis-à-vis* training courses.

The third class actually holds only one course, GMDSS practicals, belonging to courses of the Shipping group, and has assessments which are lower than average except for subject evaluations (content/objectives consistency, value of applications). In this case, we noted organisational difficulties arising from running a course for 20 trainees who had the use of only one piece of equipment. The course in question did not respect the criterion of coherence mentioned above in the first Section. Realisation of such difficulties led to immediate redesign of subsequent editions so as to prevent the situation from recurring.

Finally, the fourth and fifth class were those that gave the harshest evaluations. In particular, the fourth class, which chiefly includes courses in the 'Road transport and Shipping' groups, has lower evaluations on the part relating to practical applications, while the courses in the fifth class (chiefly 'Transversal and Air Transport' courses) produced the least satisfactory results as regards the appropriacy of course contents to learning objectives, overall evaluation, and applications.

The process ended with the phase of global checking, in which trainees expressed their degree of satisfaction with the whole training process by means of questionnaire on final satisfaction. However, the project focussed not only on the short-term results but especially on the long-term effects that such courses may have in various working contexts. A questionnaire was set to evaluate the effects of training in the workplace, in terms of opportunities for professional growth, career developments, etc., to be administered to ex-trainees and their employers.

The questionnaire on final satisfaction (Appendix 1), designed to evaluate the effectiveness and quality of the training course, considered technical and organisational aspects, time allocations to the various subjects, future professional utility and, lastly, individual course contents in terms of whether or not they corresponded to initial expectations.

The impact of the training course was subsequently examined by carrying out monitoring six months after the end of training. The effects of training in the trainees' workplace were analysed. Meetings were organised with some of the ex-trainees and attempts were made to involve their employers and/or direct superiors in order to evaluate the effects of training in each working context, in terms of job opportunities, professional growth, career development, etc.

At the time of writing, the information gathered is still being processed although, to confirm the differences already noted during the provision of training, initial results indicate substantial discrepancies among the various occupational categories surveyed, with seafarers gaining the greatest benefits from training, in terms of employment opportunities and career advancement, and public sector employers being reluctant to even take part in the meetings, clear evidence of the total lack of interest in the initiative.

Appendix 1 Evaluation questionnaire FIT PROJECT

The training scheme consisted of various elements:

♦ objectives
♦ contents / subjects handled
♦ methodology / time / sequence
♦ tutors
♦ participants

Your responses to this questionnaire will assist us in understanding:

♦ what the strengths and weaknesses of the scheme are
♦ whether and to what extent the scheme met your needs
♦ what possible changes or improvements you might want to suggest

Your comments constitute immediate feedback on the course itself and will be used as stimuli for planning other training schemes.
    Thank you for your collaboration.

FUTURE UTILITY

1. Do you think that the course you have just completed will enable you to interpret better the context in which you work?

1	2	3	4	5
a little				a lot

because _____

_____

2. To what extent do you consider this training experience concretely useful for managing your own work?

1	2	3	4	5
completely useless				very useful

because _____

_____

TECHNICAL AND ORGANISATIONAL ASPECTS

3. As regards logistics and organisation, what comments would you make?

Timetable: _____

_____

Premises: _____

_____

Teaching material: _____

_____

4. How effective was the support of tutors and course co-ordinators?

Min 1   Max 5

a)	1	2	3	4	5
b)	1	2	3	4	5
c)	1	2	3	4	5
..)	1	2	3	4	5

5. How far was your need to express yourself, ask questions and interact with tutors and other participants actually met?

1	2	3	4	5
not at all				at all times

6. Which of the course themes should have been covered in greater or lesser depth?

	Greater depth	Lesser depth	Un-changed
a)			
b)			
c)			
..)			

7. How far did the course contents respond to your expectations?

1	2	3	4	5
not at all				at all times

Why? _____

_____

8. Overall evaluation
   To what extent has the course satisfied your overall expectations?
   (give a score from '1 to 10') _____

9. Comments and suggestions

Notes

1 The data may be classified according to several discriminating criteria:

   a. Source: depending on the source, measurements may be subjective when based on an opinion, a supposition, a judgement, or objective, when they refer to an objectively measurable phenomenon without going through the actors in the training programme.

   b. Subject: data may refer to behaviour, i.e. a dynamic process, or results, i.e. performance in the static sense.

   c. Reliability: the capacity of a measurement to supply consistent results for the same phenomenon.

   d. Absence of bias: complete independence from other unknown variables which would make the measurement biased.

2 For a survey of the main training initiatives in transport and logistics in Italy, see Chapter 3.

References

Alessandrini, G. (1996), 'Modelli di valutazione dell'attività formativa : riflessioni a margine di una ricerca sul controllo della qualità dell'istruzione nella formazione continua', *Osservatorio* ISFOL.

Amietta, P.L., Amietta, F. (1989), *Valutare la formazione*, Unicopli.

Baldwin, T.T., and Ford, J.K. (1988), 'Transfer of training: a review and directions for future research', *Personnel Psychology*, Vol. 41 no. 1, pp. 63-105.

Bruscaglioni, M. (1991), 'La qualità nella formazione, Interviste AIF a testimoni privilegiati', *'FOR' (Rivista AIF per la formazione)*, no. 12, April.

Bulgarelli, A. (1991), 'Metodologie di tipo audit per l'analisi e la valutazione degli interventi di formazione', *Osservatorio* ISFOL, 4.

Clement, R., Aranda, E. (1984), 'Evaluating Management Training: a Contingency Approach', *T&D Journal*, October.

Connolly, S. (1983), 'Participant Evaluation: Finding Out How Well Training Worked', *T&D Journal*, October.

Draper, S.W., *A note on the Hawthorne Effect*, http://staff.psy.gla.ac.uk/~steve/hawth.html/

Foxon, M. (1989), 'Evaluation of training and development programs: A review of the literature', *Australian Journal of Educational Technology*, 5(2), pp. 89-104.

Hamblin, A.C. (1974), 'Evaluation of Training', *Industrial Training International*, no.5, p. 11.

Hawes, M. & Bailey, J. (1985), 'How A Validation Study of Engineering Courses Was Conducted', *Training & Development*, Vol. 4 no. 1, pp. 20-24.

Kirkpatrick, D.L. (1967), 'Evaluation of Training', Craig-Bittel (ed.), *Training and Development Handbook*, ASTD New York, McGraw-Hill.

Kirkpatrick, D.L. (1983), 'Four steps for measuring training effectiveness', *Personnel Administrator*, November.

ISFOL (1990), *Valutare l'investimento formazione*, Angeli, Milan.

Lion, C. (1996), 'Elementi per la valutazione ex-post delle attività di formazione cofinanziata dal FSE', *Osservatorio* ISFOL, 1-2.

Mayo, E. (1933), *The human problems of an industrial civilization*, New York, MacMillan, ch.3.

Mingat, A. (1991), 'Criteri di valutazione per la formazione professionale', *Professionalità*, 5.

Morris, M. (1984), 'The Evaluation of Training', *Industrial & Commercial Training*, Vol. 16 no. 2, pp. 9-16.

Quaglino, G.P. (1985), *Valutare i risultati della formazione. La formazione: criteri e metodi*, Milan, Franco Angeli.

Quaglino, G.P., Garozzi, G.P. (1987), *Il processo di formazione: dall'analisi dei bisogni alla valutazione dei risultati*, Milan, Franco Angeli.

Rae, W. L. (1985), 'How Valid Is Validation?', *Industrial & Commercial Training*, Vol. 31 no. 1, pp.15-20.

Roethlisberger, F.J., and Dickson, W.J. (1939), *Management and the Worker*, Mass. Harvard University Press, Boston.

Salinger, R., Deming, B. (1982), 'Practical Strategies for Evaluating Training', *T&D Journal*, August, pp.20.

Sordi, C. (1983), *La valutazione dei risultati della formazione. La formazione e lo sviluppo del personale*, Milan, Franco Angeli.

Tezza, E. (1992), 'La qualità della formazione professionale', *Professionalità*, no. 10.

Valentini, S. (2001), *Fare formazione con le piccole imprese*, edited by Formaper, Franco Angeli.

Vergani, A. (1991), 'La valutazione dei processi formativi', *Professionalità*, no.1, January/February.

Vergani, A. (1992), 'Una dotazione minima di indicatori a supporto della valutazione', *Professionalità*, no. 7.

Vergani, A. (1994), 'La qualità della formazione: pensarla, progettarla e realizzarla', *Skill, 9*.

Vergani, A. (1995), 'Valutazione dell'efficacia degli interventi formativi', *Professionalità*, no. 30.

Vergani, A. (1995-1997), 'La valutazione di qualità nella formazione: esperienze e problemi in prospettiva istituzionale e aziendale', *Cesos*.

Vergani, A. (1997), 'La valutazione di qualità e l'analisi costi-benefici in iniziative e strutture dedicate alla formazione professionale', *Cesos*.

Warr, (1972), 'Evaluating', *An Introductory Course*.

Appendix

Web sites of Logistics and Transport Training Institutions in the European Union

Web site Legend

Type of organisation	Institutional (University, Public Research Centres, NGOs); Private (Consulting firms, Private Training firms, Private Research Centres, etc.)
Mode of transport specialisation	Maritime; Road; Air: Rail; All
Type of training	Master; Short course; Stage; Diploma
Main topics	Management; Logistics; Distribution; IT/e-business; etc.
Other activities	Consultancy; Research
Target	Professionals/Managers; Blue collar workers; Operative workers; Post-graduate or Undergraduate students; All
Downloadable material	Abstracts; Application material; Articles or Book reviews; Brochures; Information; Newsletter; Legislation/Regulation; Papers; Power Point Presentations; Press releases; Publications; Reports
Other services	Links to transportation/logistics web sites; Library access; Student Services; Business Services; Magazine
Web site wealth of information	* (poor); ** (fair); *** (good)
Web site quality design	* (poor); ** (fair); *** (good); (aesthetics balanced with usability; navigational aids; layout)

BELGIUM

Cordis

Web site	http://www.cordis.lu/transport/src/master.htm
Type of organisation	Institutional
Mode of transport specialisation	Road
Typology of training	Master
Main topics	Management; Logistics; Distribution
Other activities	Research
Target	All
Downloadable material	Power Point Presentations; Publications
Other services	Links to transportation/logistics web sites
Web site wealth of information	**
Web site quality design	*

Institute of Transport and Maritime Management Antwerp

Web site	http://www.ruca.ua.ac.be/itmma/welcome.html
Type of organisation	Institutional
Mode of transport specialisation	Maritime; All
Typology of training	Master; Short course
Main topics	Management; Logistics; IT/e-business
Other activities	Research
Target	Professionals/Managers; Post-graduate
Downloadable material	Power Point Presentations
Other services	Links to transportation; Library access
Web site wealth of information	*
Web site quality design	**

FRANCE

AFT-IFTIM

Web site	http://www.aft-iftim.com
Type of organisation	Private
Mode of transport specialisation	All
Typology of training	Master "Logistic & Supply Chain Management"; Short courses; Diploma
Main topics	Management ; Logistic; Distribution
Other activities	Consultancy; Research
Target	All
Downloadable material	Papers; Reports
Other services	Links to transportation/logistics web sites
Web site wealth of information	**
Web site quality design	***

Bordeaux School of Management

Web site	www.esc.bordeaux-bs.edu
Type of organisation	Institutional
Mode of transport specialisation	All
Typology of training	Master "European Logistics & Supply Chain Management"; Stage
Main topics	Management; Logistics
Other activities	Consultancy
Target	Post-graduate
Downloadable material	Power Point Presentations
Other services	Research; Student Services
Web site wealth of information	**
Web site quality design	**

ESILOG

Web site	http://www.esidec.fr/formation
Type of organisation	Private
Mode of transport specialisation	All
Typology of training	Master
Main topics	Logistics; Management
Other activities	Consultancy; Research
Target	Post-graduate students; Professionals/Managers
Downloadable material	Power Point Presentations
Other services	Links to transportation/logistics web sites; Library access
Web site wealth of information	*
Web site quality design	*

Groupe Sup de Co Montpellier

Web site	http://www.supco-montpellier.fr/
Type of organisation	Institutional
Mode of transport specialisation	All
Typology of training	Master "Logistics & Supply Chain Management"
Main topics	Logistics; Distribution; Management
Other activities	Consultancy
Target	Professionals/Managers; Post-graduate
Downloadable material	Power Point Presentations
Other services	
Web site wealth of information	**
Web site quality design	**

L'Université d'Aix-Marseille (Marseille)

Web site	http://www.up.univ-mrs.fr/
Type of organisation	Institutional
Mode of transport specialisation	All
Typology of training	Master "Logistics"
Main topics	Logistics; Distribution; Management
Other activities	Consultancy
Target	Professionals/Managers; Blue collar workers; Post-graduate
Downloadable material	Power Point Presentations
Other services	Research; Student Services
Web site wealth of information	**
Web site quality design	***

PROMOTRANS

Web site	http://www.promotrans.asso.fr/
Type of organisation	Private
Mode of transport specialisation	Road
Typology of training	Master; Short courses; Stages
Main topics	Logistics ; Management
Other activities	Consultancy; Research
Target	All
Downloadable material	Power Point Presentations
Other services	Links to transportation/logistics web sites; Library access
Web site wealth of information	**
Web site quality design	**

GERMANY

Dresden University of Technology (Dresden)

In collaboration with: Université du Havre (Le Havre) – Universiteit Ghent (Ghent) – Université de Liège (Liège) – Universidad de Cantabria (Santander)

Web site	http://www.tu-dresden.de
Type of organisation	Institutional
Mode of transport specialisation	All
Typology of training	Master "European Master in Transport & Logistics"
Main topics	Logistics
Other activities	Consultancy
Target	All
Downloadable material	Power Point Presentations
Other services	Student Services
Web site wealth of information	*
Web site quality design	*

GREECE

Airline Services Training

Web site	http://www.hol.gr/business/ast/profile.htm
Type of organisation	Institutional
Mode of transport specialisation	Air
Typology of training	Short courses; Diploma
Main topics	Logistics; Distribution
Other activities	Consultancy
Target	All
Downloadable material	Power Point Presentations
Other services	Library access
Web site wealth of information	**
Web site quality design	**

IRELAND

The Chartered Institute of Transport in Ireland

Web site	http://www.citi.ie/citi_i.htm
Type of organisation	Institutional
Mode of transport specialisation	All
Typology of training	Short Course; Diploma
Main topics	Logistics; Management; Distribution
Other activities	Research
Target	Professionals/ Managers; Blue collar workers
Downloadable material	Power Point Presentations
Other services	Links to transportation/logistics web sites; Library access
Web site wealth of information	*
Web site quality design	*

NETHERLANDS

Erasmus University of Rotterdam

Web site	http://www.eur.nl/eur-uk/education/ postgraduate/maritime.html
Type of organisation	Institutional
Mode of transport specialisation	Maritime; All
Typology of training	Master
Main topics	Distribution; Logistics
Other activities	Research
Target	Post-graduate; Professionals/Managers
Downloadable material	Power Point Presentations
Other services	Links to transportation/logistics web sites; Library access
Web site wealth of information	***
Web site quality design	***

International Management Institute

Web site	http://www.millian.nl/206.htm
Type of organisation	Institutional
Mode of transport specialisation	All
Typology of training	Master
Main topics	Distribution; Logistics; Management
Other activities	Consultancy; Research
Target	Post-graduate; Professionals/Managers
Downloadable material	Power Point Presentations
Other services	Links to transportation/logistics web sites; Library access
Web site wealth of information	*
Web site quality design	**

NEA

Web site	http://www.nea.nl/
Type of organisation	Private
Mode of transport specialisation	All
Typology of training	Short Course; Master
Main topics	Distribution; Logistics
Other activities	Consultancy; Research
Target	All
Downloadable material	Reports; Legislation/Regulation
Other services	Links to transportation/logistics web sites
Web site wealth of information	**
Web site quality design	*

Shipping and Transport College

Web site	http://www.stc-r.nl/stc_bedryf/ bedryf_dms.htm
Type of organisation	Institutional
Mode of transport specialisation	Maritime
Typology of training	Diploma
Main topics	IT/e-business; Distribution; Logistics
Other activities	Consultancy; Research
Target	Post-graduate; Professionals/Managers
Downloadable material	Power Point Presentations; Brochures
Other services	Links to transportation/logistics web sites; Library access
Web site wealth of information	*
Web site quality design	**

PORTUGAL

Instituto Superior Técnico

Web site	http://www.ist.utl.pt/uk/teaching/masters/ transport.html
Type of organisation	Institutional
Mode of transport specialisation	All
Typology of training	Master
Main topics	Management; Logistics; Distribution
Other activities	Research
Target	Post-graduate
Downloadable material	Power Point Presentations
Other services	Links to transportation/logistics web sites; Library access
Web site wealth of information	*
Web site quality design	*

SPAIN

Centro Espanol de Logistica

Web site	http:/www.cel-logistica.org/
Type of organisation	Private
Mode of transport specialisation	All
Typology of training	Short courses
Main topics	Logistics; Distribution
Other activities	Consultancy
Target	All
Downloadable material	Power Point Presentations; Articles
Other services	Links to transportation/logistics web sites; Library access
Web site wealth of information	**
Web site quality design	**

SWEDEN

Chalmers University of Technology

Web site	Http://www.chalmers.se/Home-E.html
Type of organisation	Institutional
Mode of transport specialisation	All
Typology of training	Master "Management of Logistics and Transportation"
Main topics	Management; Logistics
Other activities	Consultancy
Target	Post-graduate
Downloadable material	Power Point Presentations; Abstracts
Other services	Research
Web site wealth of information	**
Web site quality design	**

UNITED KINGDOM

Cranfield University

Web site	http://www.cranfield.ac.uk
Type of organisation	Institutional
Mode of transport specialisation	All
Typology of training	Master "Logistic & Supply Chain Management"; Course
Main topics	Management; Logistics; IT/e-business; Distribution
Other activities	Consultancy; Research
Target	Post-graduate; Blue collar workers
Downloadable material	Papers
Other services	Business Services; Library access
Web site wealth of information	**
Web site quality design	**

Freight Transport Association

Web site	http://www.fta.co.uk/services/training.htm
Type of organisation	Private
Mode of transport specialisation	All
Typology of training	Master; Diploma
Main topics	Management; Logistics, Distribution
Other activities	Consultancy; Research
Target	All
Downloadable material	Information; Press releases
Other services	Links to transportation/logistics web sites; Library access
Web site wealth of information	**
Web site quality design	*

Heriot-Watt University (Edinburgh)

Web site	http://www.hw.ac.uk
Type of organisation	Institutional
Mode of transport specialisation	All
Typology of training	Master "Logistic and Supply Chain Management"
Main topics	Management; Logistics
Other activities	Consultancy
Target	All
Downloadable material	Brochures; Application material
Other services	Library access; Business Services
Web site wealth of information	***
Web site quality design	**

Middlesex University Business School

Web site	http://www.mdx.ac.uk/www/roadtraffic/welcome.htm
Type of organisation	Institutional
Mode of transport specialisation	Road transport
Typology of training	Diploma; Master
Main topics	IT/e-business; Management
Other activities	Research
Target	Post-graduate;
Downloadable material	Power Point Presentations
Other services	Links to transportation/logistics web sites; Library access
Web site wealth of information	*
Web site quality design	*

National Training Institute LLC

Web site	http://www.tawoos.com/nti/nti2.htm
Type of organisation	Private
Mode of transport specialisation	Maritime; Roa
Typology of training	Master
Main topics	Management; Logistics
Other activities	Research
Target	Blue collar workers; All
Downloadable material	Power Point Presentations
Other services	Links to transportation/logistics web sites
Web site wealth of information	*
Web site quality design	*

The Institute of Logistics and Transport

Web site	http://www.iolt.org.uk/training/training.htm
Type of organisation	Institutional
Mode of transport specialisation	All
Typology of training	Short Courses; Diploma
Main topics	Logistics; Transport; Management
Other activities	Consultancy; Research
Target	Professionals/Managers; Post-graduate; Blue collar workers
Downloadable material	Book reviews; Power Point Presentations
Other services	Links to transportation/logistics web sites; Library access
Web site wealth of information	***
Web site quality design	***

The University of York – Institute of Railway Studies

Web site	http://www.york.ac.uk/inst/irs
Type of organisation	Institutional
Mode of transport specialisation	Railway
Typology of training	Short Course; Master; Diploma
Main topics	Logistics; Management
Other activities	Research
Target	Professionals/Managers; Blue collar workers; Post-graduate
Downloadable material	Papers; Power Point Presentations
Other services	Links to transportation/logistics web sites
Web site wealth of information	**
Web site quality design	*

University of Newcastle

Web site	http://www.ncl.ac.uk/torg
Type of organisation	Institutional
Mode of transport specialisation	All
Typology of training	Master; Diploma
Main topics	Management; Logistics; IT/e-business
Other activities	Research
Target	Post-graduate; Professionals/Managers
Downloadable material	Papers; Reports
Other services	Links to transportation
Web site wealth of information	**
Web site quality design	**

University of Wales (Cardiff)

Web site	http://www.cardiff.ac.uk
Type of organisation	Institutional
Mode of transport specialisation	All
Typology of training	Master "International Transport" – "Supply Chain Management"
Main topics	Logistics; Management
Other activities	Consultancy
Target	Professionals/Managers; Post-graduate
Downloadable material	Power Point Presentations; project reports
Other services	Magazine; Business Services
Web site wealth of information	***
Web site quality design	***

University of Westminster (London)

Web site	http://www.wmin.ac.uk
Type of organisation	Institutional
Mode of transport specialisation	All
Typology of training	Master "European Logistics, Transport & Distribution" – "Transport Planning & Management"
Main topics	Logistics; Distribution; Management
Other activities	Consultancy; Research
Target	Professionals/Managers; Post-graduate
Downloadable material	Power Point Presentations
Other services	Student Services; Business Services
Web site wealth of information	***
Web site quality design	**

Index